"CAFÉ PANORAMA"
San Pedro La Laguna, Guatemala

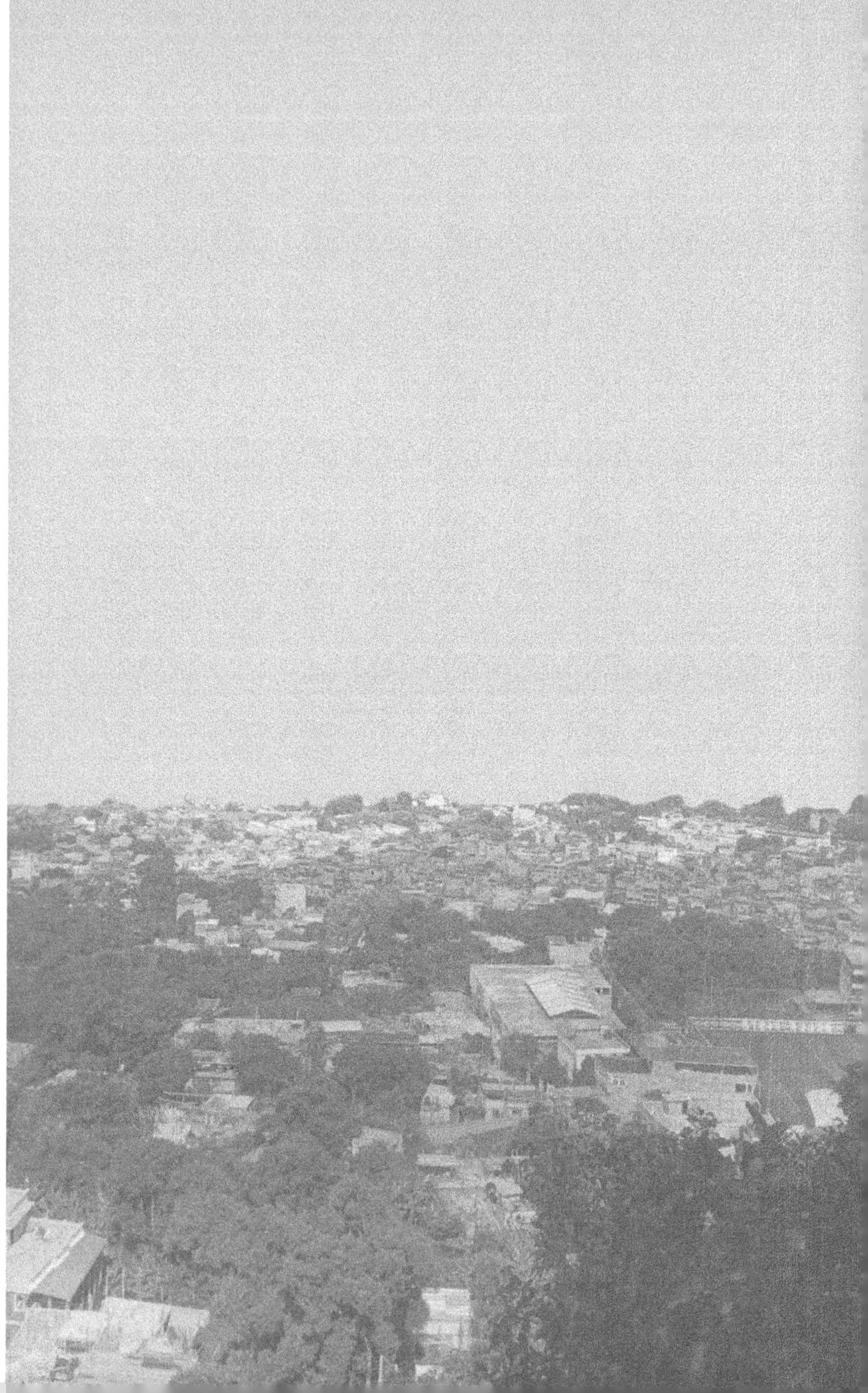

A FAIRY GUIDE TO
LAKE ATITLAN, GUATEMALA

AUTHOR

Lady Victoria Rose

Rose & Stone Media

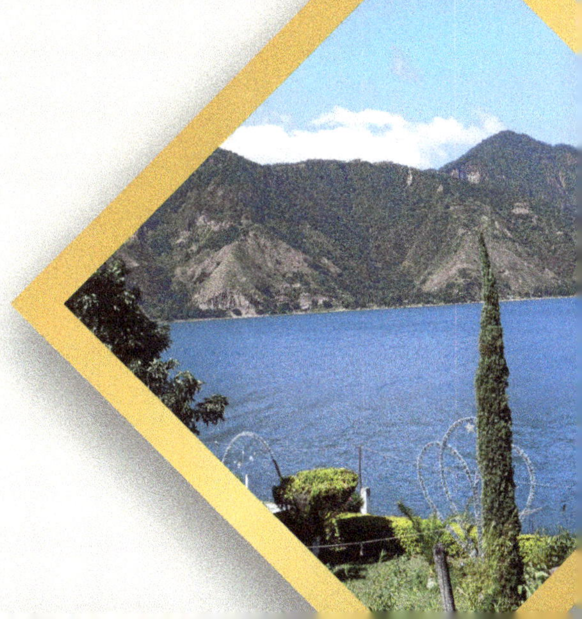

This book is for entertainment,
it is from the author's own personal experience and perspective, she is just a fairy wandering the world. All information is to the best of her knowledge and is not guaranteed in any form, nor a substitute for verified information from Journalistic, governmental, or other sources.

Please use discretion and do personal research when traveling anywhere.
All persons, places, things, and ideas mentioned in this book are appreciated and likely not figments of imagination.

For more information, cooperation, commentary, offers of chocolate tastings, or other adventures, please message her @TheCozyFairyCollection on Substack, she always loves a chat!

RoseAndStoneMedia.com

Written by Lady Victoria Rose

Photos by Lady Victoria Rose, used with permission, or public domain
Editing by Sérgio Stone

ISBN13: 978-1-967007-19-6 (trade paperback)
LCCN: 2026902260

First Edition

Copyright 2025
by
Rose & Stone Media
Tequesta, FL

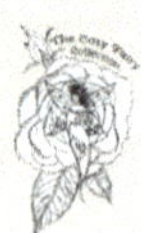

The Cozy Fairy Collection

10 9 8 7 6 5 4 3 2

CONTENTS

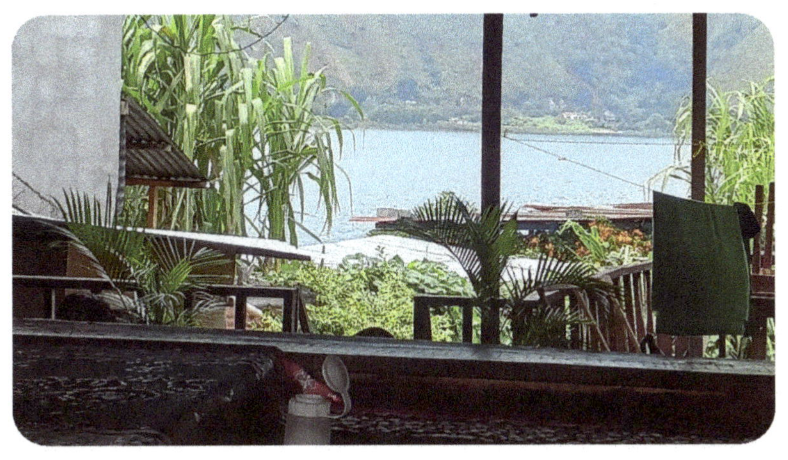

A JOURNEY INTO THE JUNGLE

Creative & Restorative Retreat among an Ancient Civilization

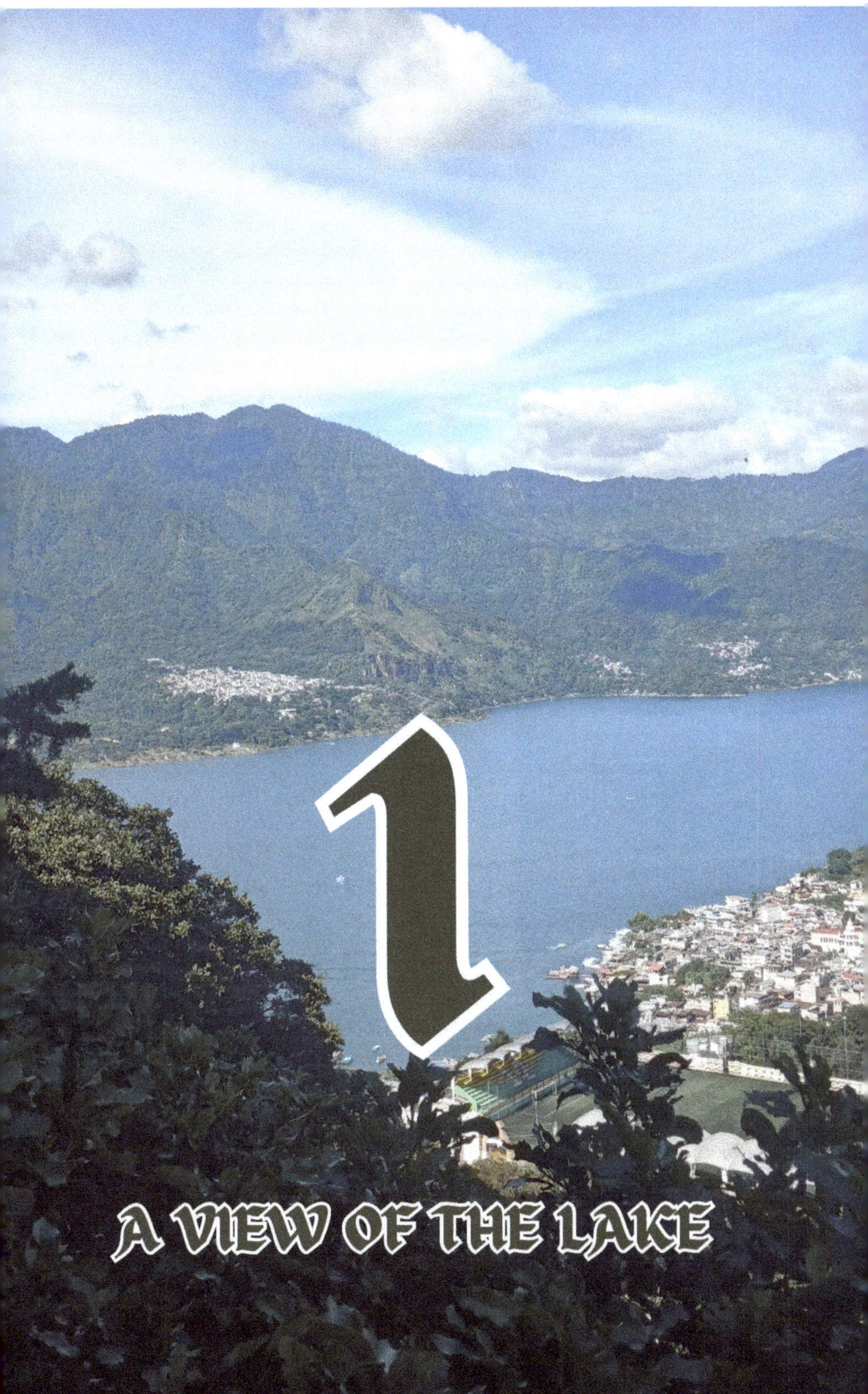
1
A VIEW OF THE LAKE

WHERE IN THE WORLD IS SAN PEDRO?

San Pedro is a beautiful little town on the edge of Lake Atitlan, Guatemala. The smallness of the town is made up for by the beauty of the surroundings & the peacefulness of the lifestyle. If you desire solitude, silence, and endless stars at night, this is the perfect place.

There are a number of villiages surrounding the lake, one of the largest being San Marcos, the top tourist area, but if you'd like a more quiet retreat and connection to the local culture, San Pedro is a far better option.

Everything essential to life is there, and frankly, after a few days you won't care about anything else anyway, enjoying the beauty of the constant flowers, butterflies, and movement of the water on the lake.

To be honest, half the reason for staying might be the day long adventure it takes to get there from Guatemala City!

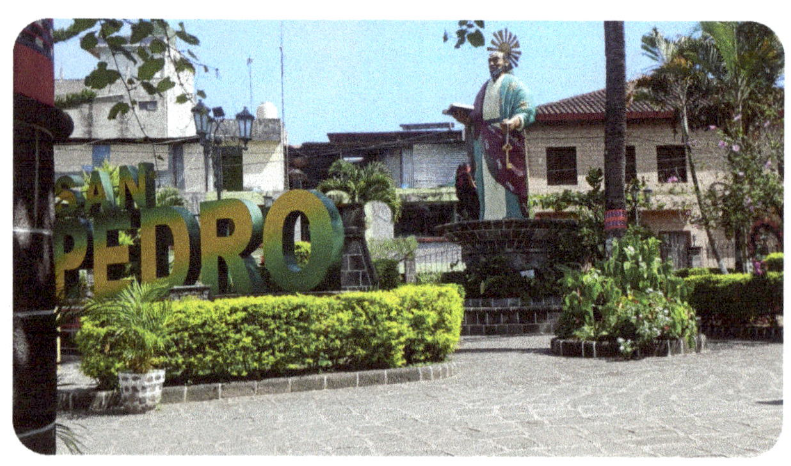

HOW I ENDED UP AT THE LAKE

After my time in Mexico, I was looking for other areas in Latin America to visit, under the delusion I'd work more on my Spanish (which is still going shamefully slow, but I've also written three books in a year, so that might have an impact on my brain space as well!)

I typically start with looking at places to stay & things to do in a region, and after exploring options in Costa Rica & Belize, nothing truly inspiring came up. Looking over Airbnb options in Guatemala, I found it: The Fairy Cottage!

Not actually what the place was called, but it was absolutely perfect for a little creative writng retreat before going back to Mexico. A cozy little cabin with a view of gardens & the lake, beautifully decorated with raw wood furniture & local paintings, it was a dream come true (it also turned out to have a talkative resident kitty, who became a dear friend in my time there).

I booked everything, finished my US to-do list, and headed into the jungle. Thank all the heavens I only brought one suitcase! It seems I took the long route, even though there really is no short route to the lake, by doing a shuttle, then a boat, then a Tuktuk, and I was genuinely wondering if I'd need a donkey to get through the last part of the journey. Instead I overpaid the driver to help me carry everything down the winding hillside to the cottage. I'm not a heavy packer, but I do work on the road and must have some kind of supplies with me.
But San Pedro for others? If you don't need it, don't bring it!

I met a number of fellow travelers at Idea Connection- one of the top 2 cafes in town for Wifi, food, drinks, and comfy hangout spaces- and soon had a merry band of free-spirited ladies causing delightful chaos all around town. My now-husband also came to visit while I was there, which certainly added to the fun!

My solo creative retreat turned into a much more deeply needed experience of healing and reconnecting with nature, as I found a clearer path for my future goals.

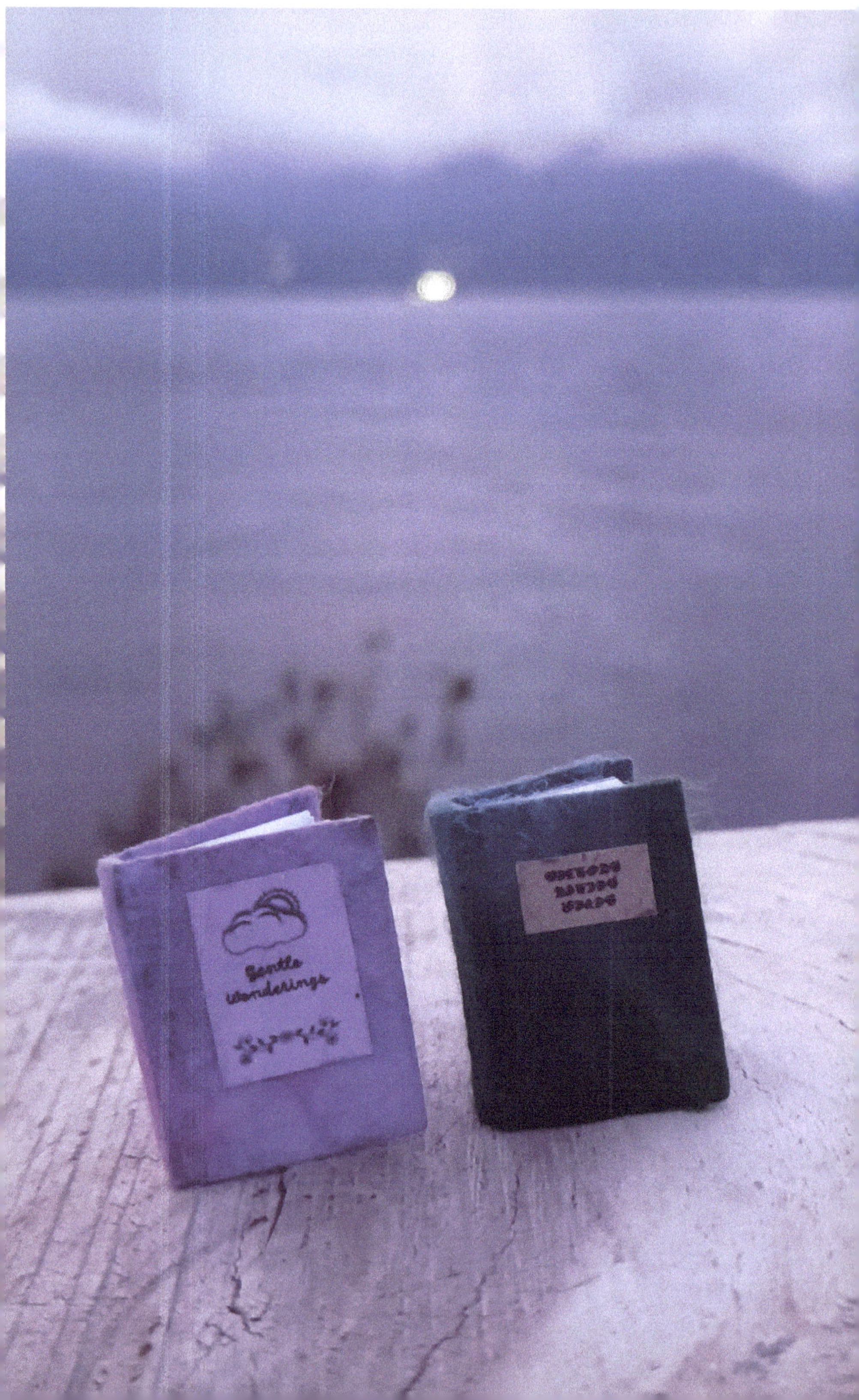
Gentle
Wanderings

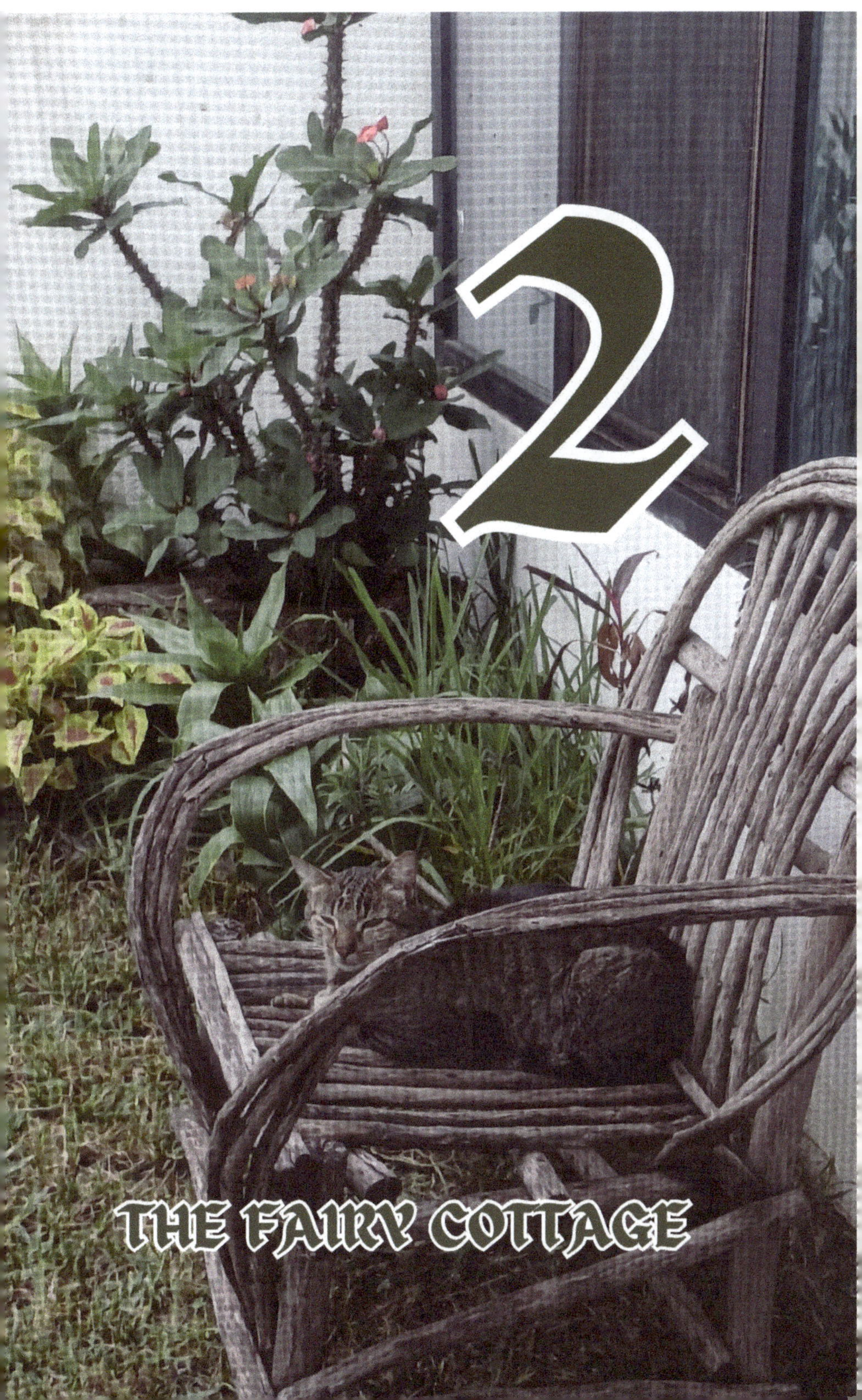

2
THE FAIRY COTTAGE

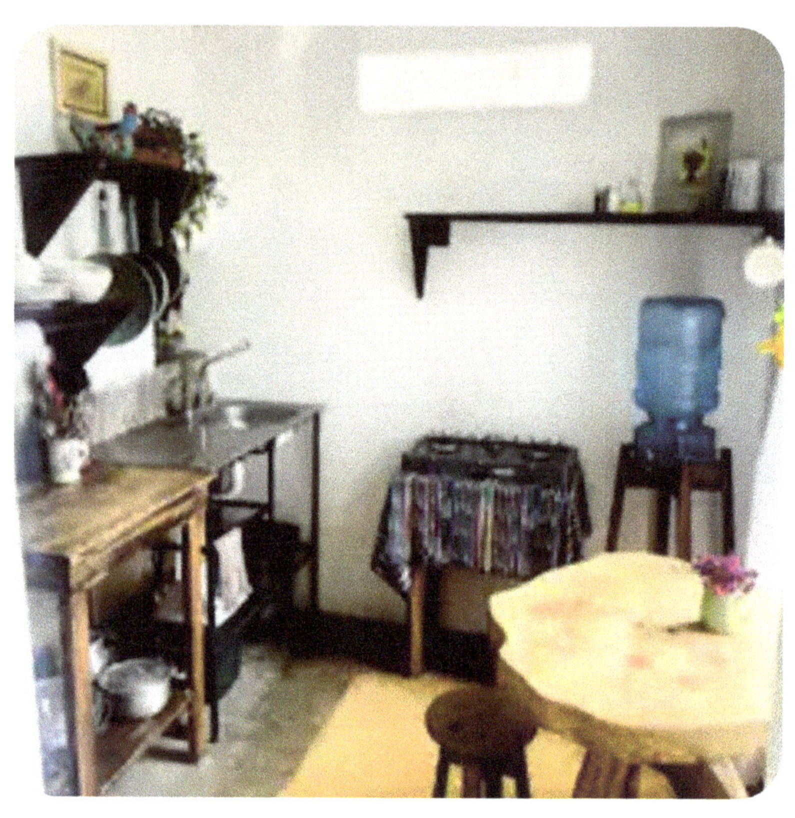

THE FAIRY COTTAGE

Simply called "The Lakehouse" on Airbnb, hosts Alex & Ashley are expats who help locals set up vacation homes for visitors.
This place was perfect as a creative retreat (or a nice honeymoon). It's about a 10 minute walk into town, so it's quiet, beautiful, & has everything you need for a peaceful experience.

Along with the sweetest little welcome sign, they made sure water, coffee, basic cooking supplies like oil & eggs were available. There's housekeeping 2x per month for long stays & laundry delivery available.

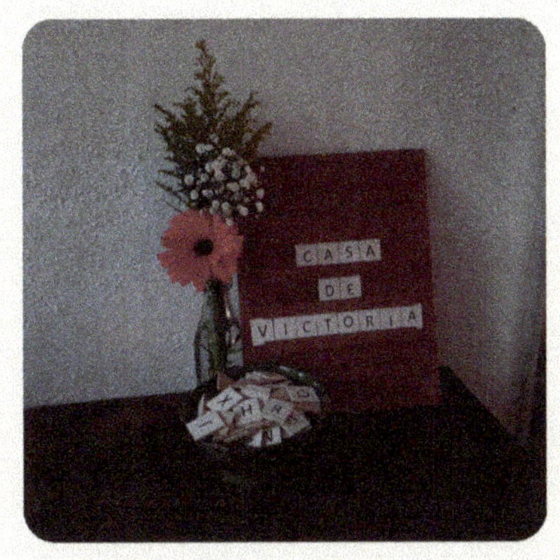

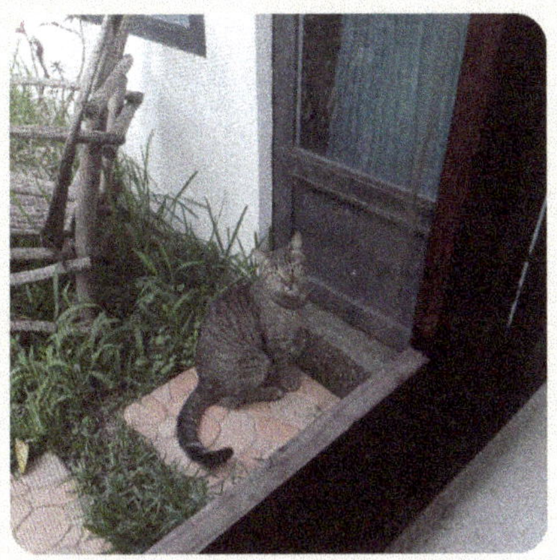

This furry scoudrel showed up within the first few hours I was there. He belonged to one of the neighbors, but clearly knew how to keep his coat fluffy and tummy full, because he yowled until I opened the door, walked right in and hung out until he deemed dinner to be good enough.
I absolutely adored him, and spoiled him like he was my own.

The singular downside to the cottage, and Guatemala as a whole, is the Spider n' Scorpion population. Technically none of them are harmful, but for someone with arachnaphobia as powerful as mine, well, I'm not going to win any prizes for "Peace with all Creatures" spiritual enlightment anytime soon. It was war, and I demolished my enemy brutally. Frying pans & chemical warfare were involved.

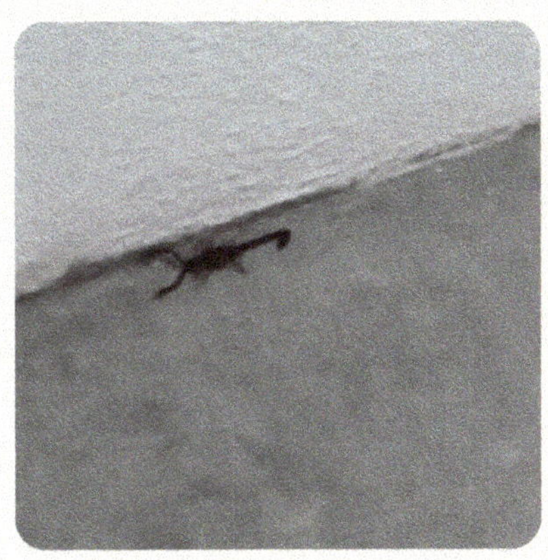

The Cottage was very well
decorated, the bathroom
had a great shower with
good hot water, and the bed
was very comfy!

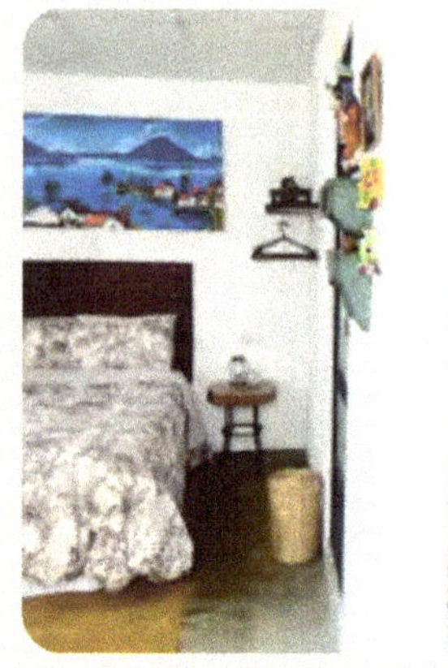
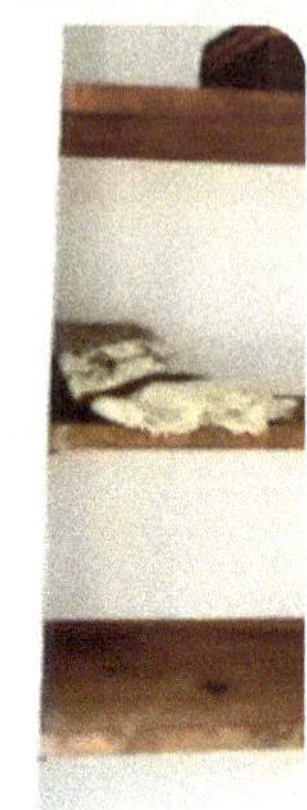

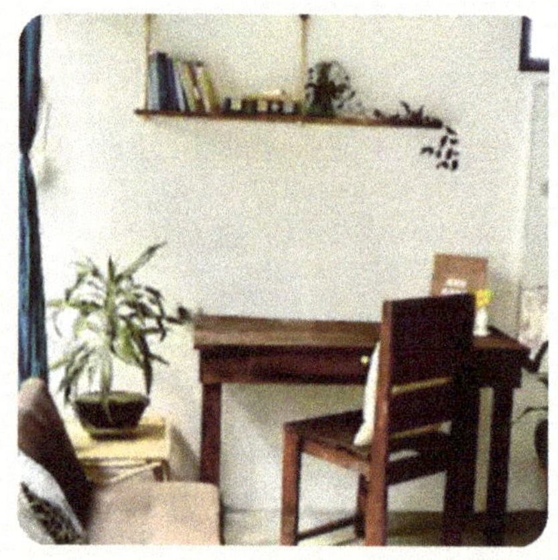

I spent many an hour here
working on art and new
stories, cuddling my kitty
friend.

At the top of the hill by the
cottage is a wonderful Italian
restaurant with homemade
pasta & a beautiful view. On
days I didn't want to walk into
town, I'd have dinner here,
read, and watch the clouds
move over the Lake.

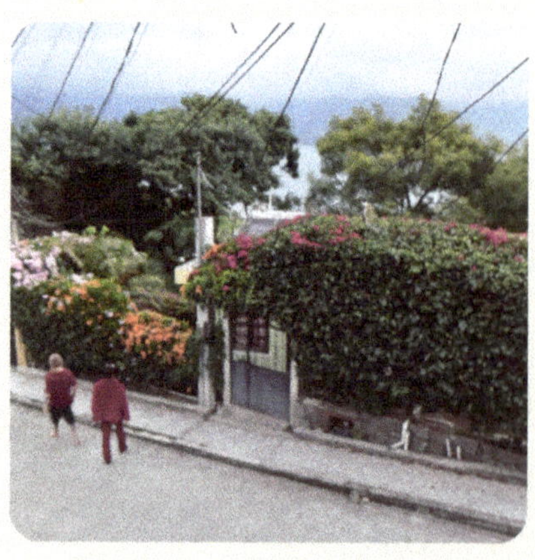

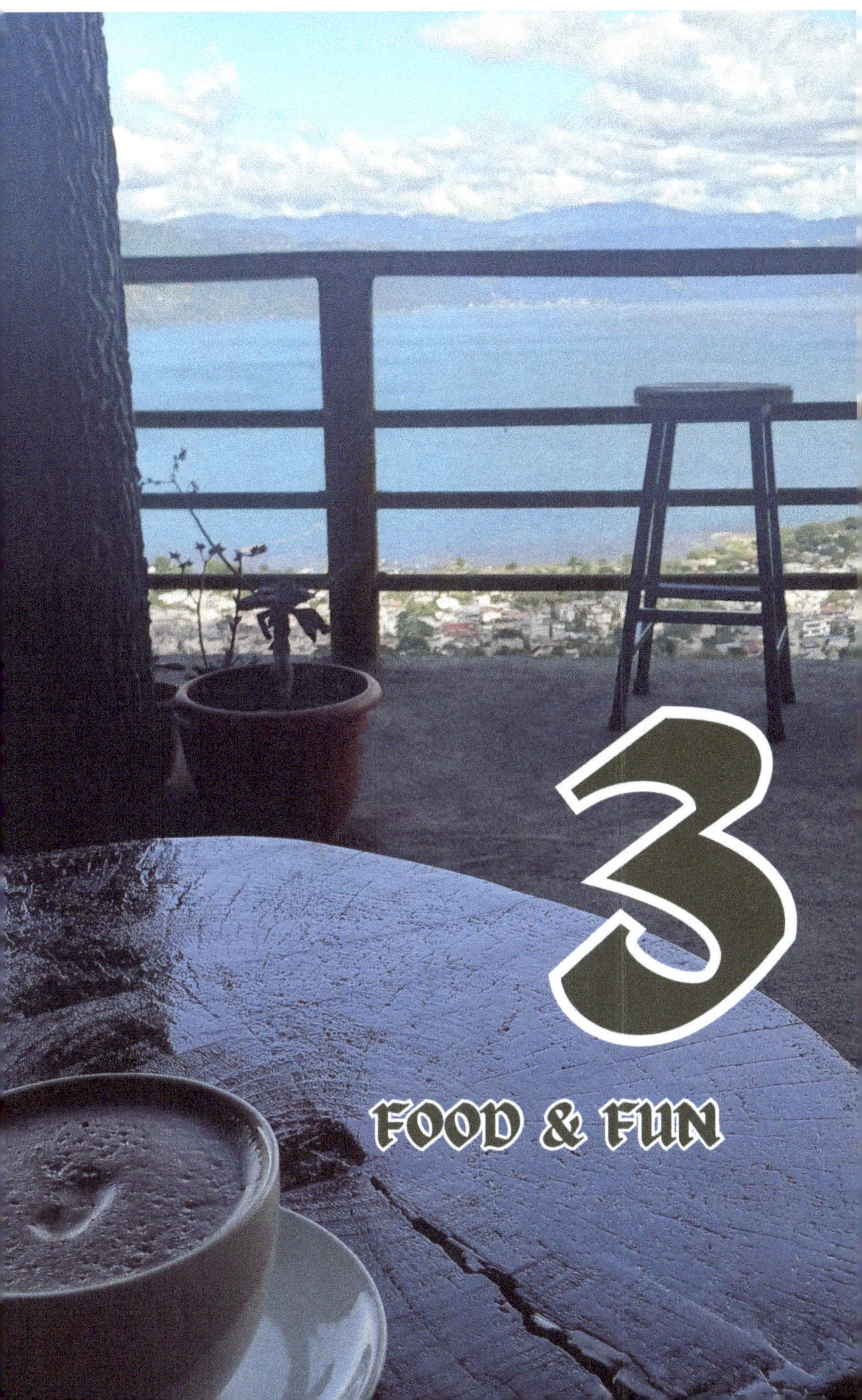

3
FOOD & FUN

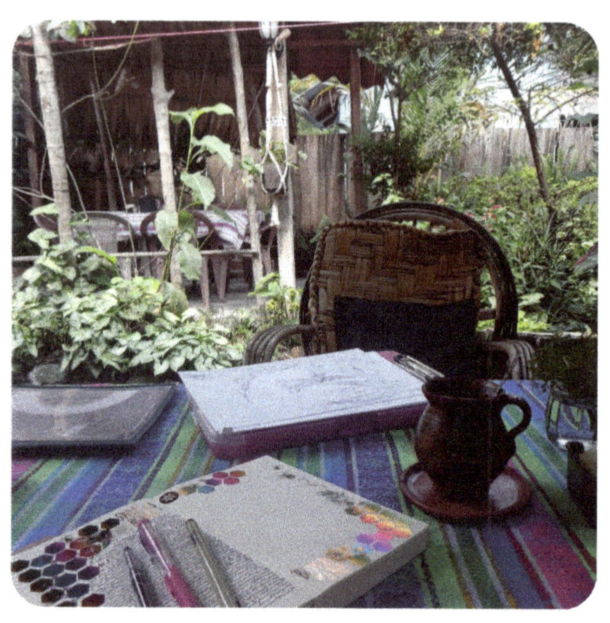

IDEA CONNECTION CAFE

There is a lot of good food in San Pedro, but anyone who stays for more than a week ends up at *Idea Connection*. It has the best Wifi, best cookies, and best general hangout vibes in the area. While *Tornados* has better food & is generally more comfortable & pretty, *Idea Connection* just invites, well, connections. I met new people basically every time I visited.

Some of my favorite memories, of Guatemala & my life, are of working on my illustrations & having ridiculous conversations with the Cast of Characters that populates San Pedro at all times.

Also, while the general food here ranges from excellent to disappointing depending who is in the kitchen, as anywhere, the
"Breakfast Tipico"
-pictured on the next page- is absolutely perfect. I actually do my best to replicate it at home as often as possible. The combination of bread, eggs, beans, cheese, fruit, fried platanos, and avocado is heaven on a plate, nutrition & palate wise.

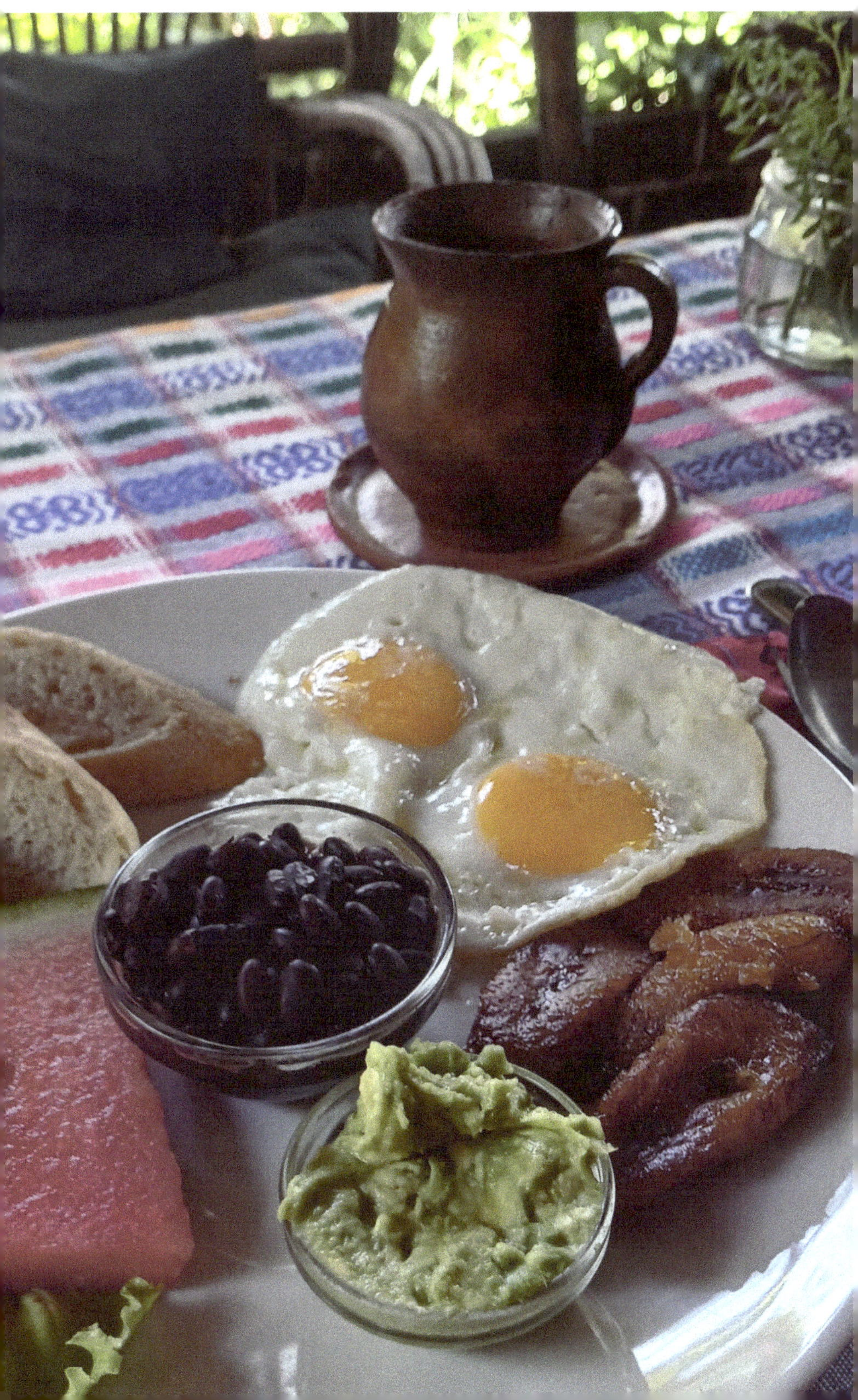

Most of my pictures at Idea
Connection are of my art,
since I spent most of my time
there sketching & painting
for my next book.

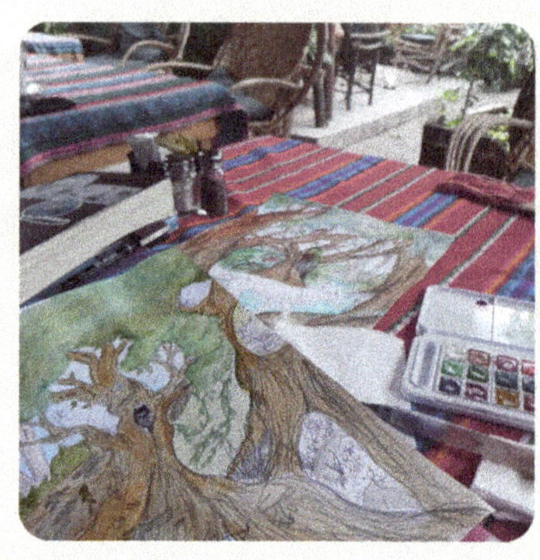

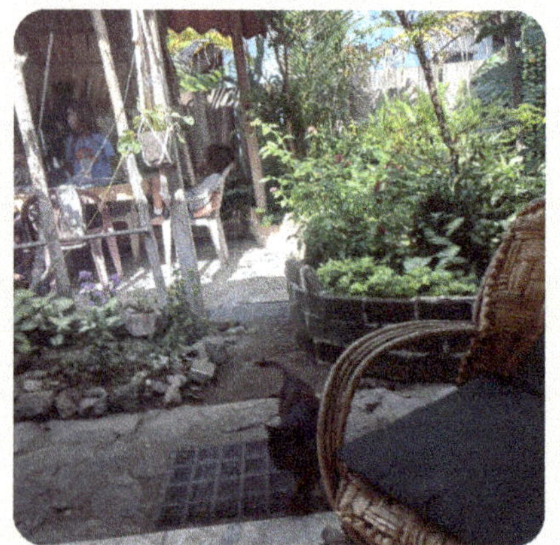

There was a very friendly,
incredibly old cat when I was
there, who'd sit in the garden
and watch the butterflies &
hummingbirds with us.

One of my favorite parts
about the whole town was
that it felt like there were
flowers absolutely
everywhere. Perfec for doing
photos of my fairy sized
books!

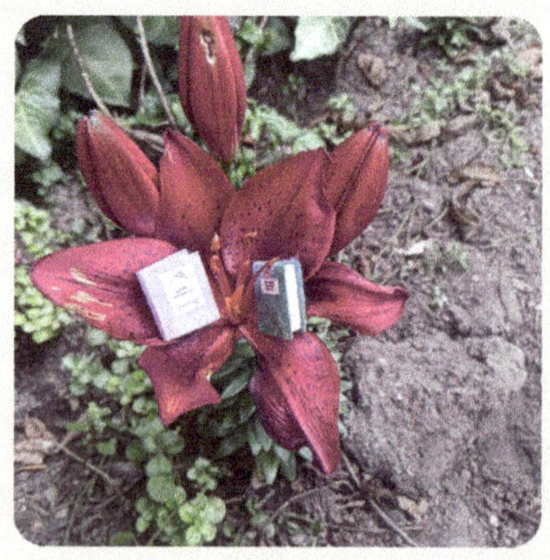

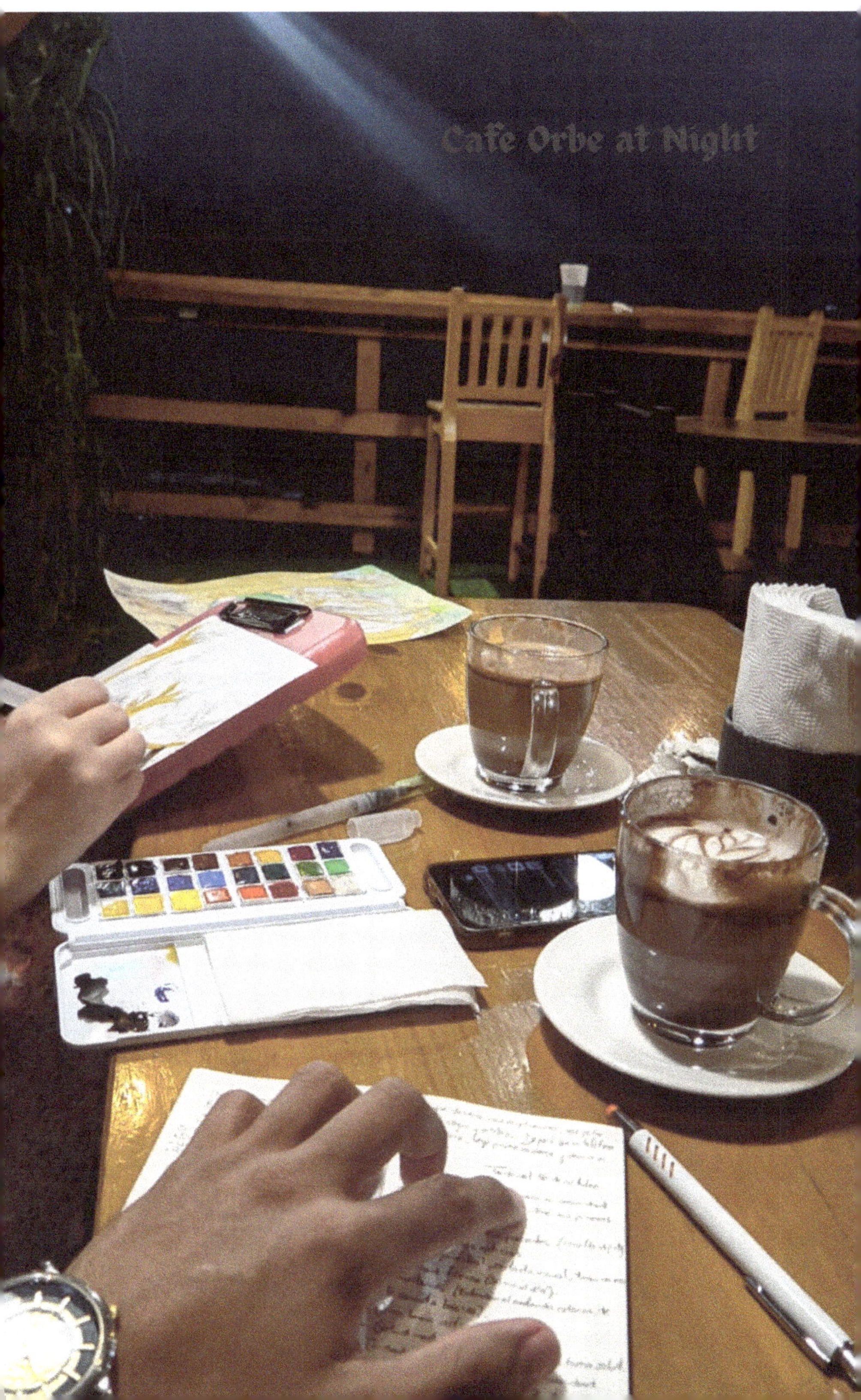
Cafe Orbe at Night

CAFE ORBE

Worth an honorable mention because of how often I was there; this place was closest to my cottage, and definitely had the best hot chocolate in town. I recommend the Cardamom or the Mint.

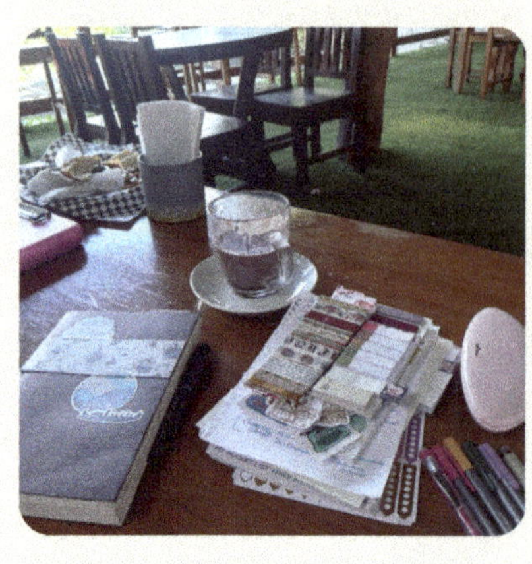

TASTY PLATES

Meat was slightly expensive and difficult to come by at most of the cafes, etc, with the occasional exception of chicken. So while I don't often eat this way, I was happy that Orbe's hamburger & fries was also decent.

VIEW OF MAJESTY

While this cafe was not my favorite, it was decent, the real worthwhile experience here is the incredible view from the second level. This became another favorite place to work, because how could I not be inspired looking at glorious mountains & endless lake?

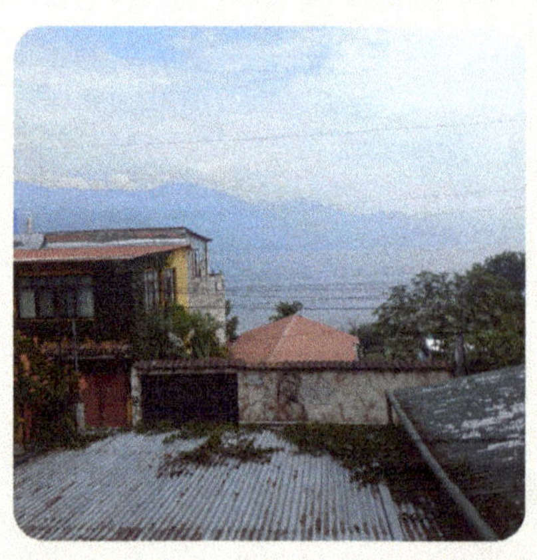

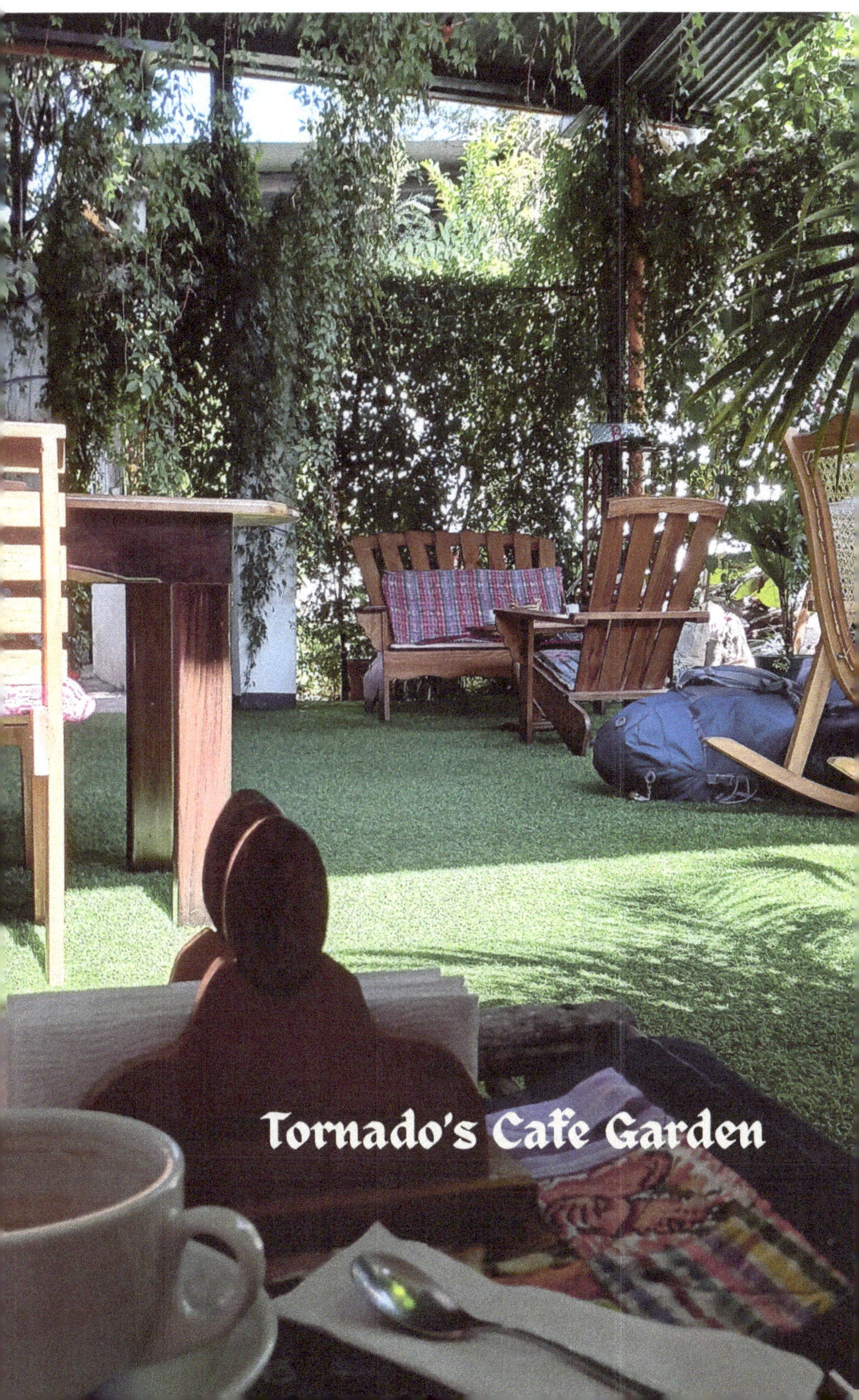
Tornado's Cafe Garden

TORNADO'S
THE BEST CAFE IN SAN PEDRO, DEFINITELY TOP RANKING IN THE WORLD

If *Idea Connecion* is where everyone ends up, *Tornado's* is only for people in "the know". It is absolutely the best cafe in the area, simply because it is the most comfortable place I've ever been.

The tiny front door leads to a whole world; a huge garden space, scattered tables, chairs, and couches makes it feel like entering a fairy garden, separate from the rest of the world. Butterflies are always nearby, playing in the flowers that drape from the framing over the whole place.

It also has the best coffee in the area, for the true coffee lovers. The family who owns the cafe produces it themselves on a farm that has been tended by them for four generations. You can buy it by the kilo, and they are branching into international distribution.

Food wise, it's more limited than *Idea Connection*, but that doesn't matter when the signature dish- Chicken quesadilla- is the best thing I've ever tasted. Seriously, I still dream about whatever magic and spice marinade they used. At one point, the owner couldn't help but laugh when a whole table of us just ordered quesadillas and hot chocolate.

My favorite spot was the couch in the very back, tucked under a staircase, since sometimes we'd get afternoon showers & I didn't want my artwork getting wet. It also has the best view of the whole garden & was big enough to stretch out my legs.

Honestly I wish I'd taken more pictures of the place, but truly I'd forget how to be a working professional when I was there, just enjoying life, food, and butterflies.

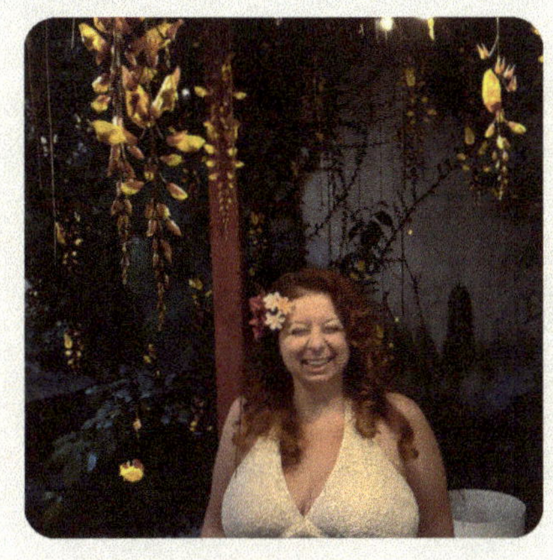

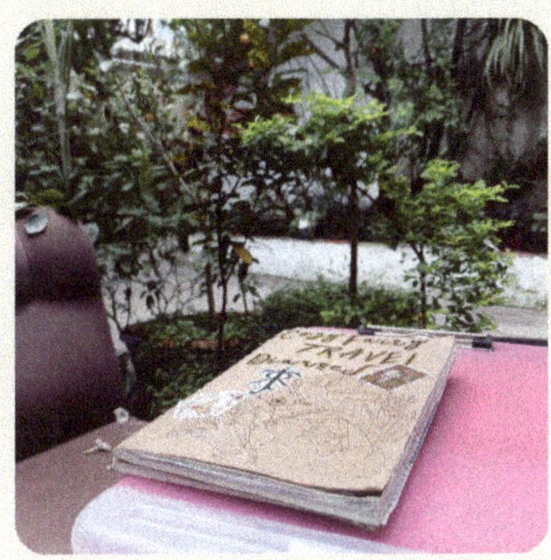

One of the rare times I sat at a table at Tornado's instead of my couch, it was a lovely view, and I was visited by multiple hummingbirds.

View from my couch, my favorite place in Guatemala. I will forever be seeking a cafe work spot equally as perfect.

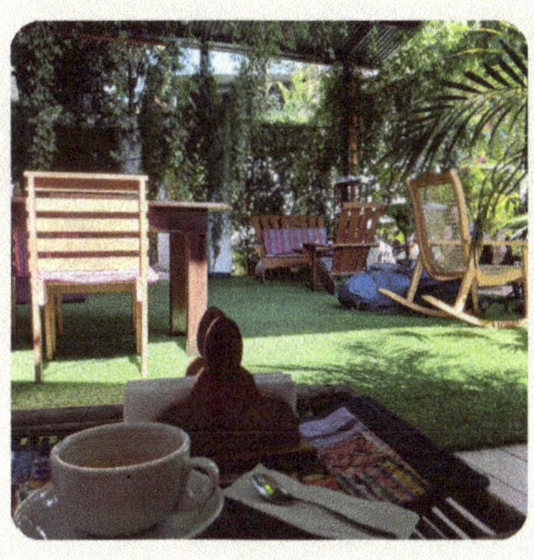

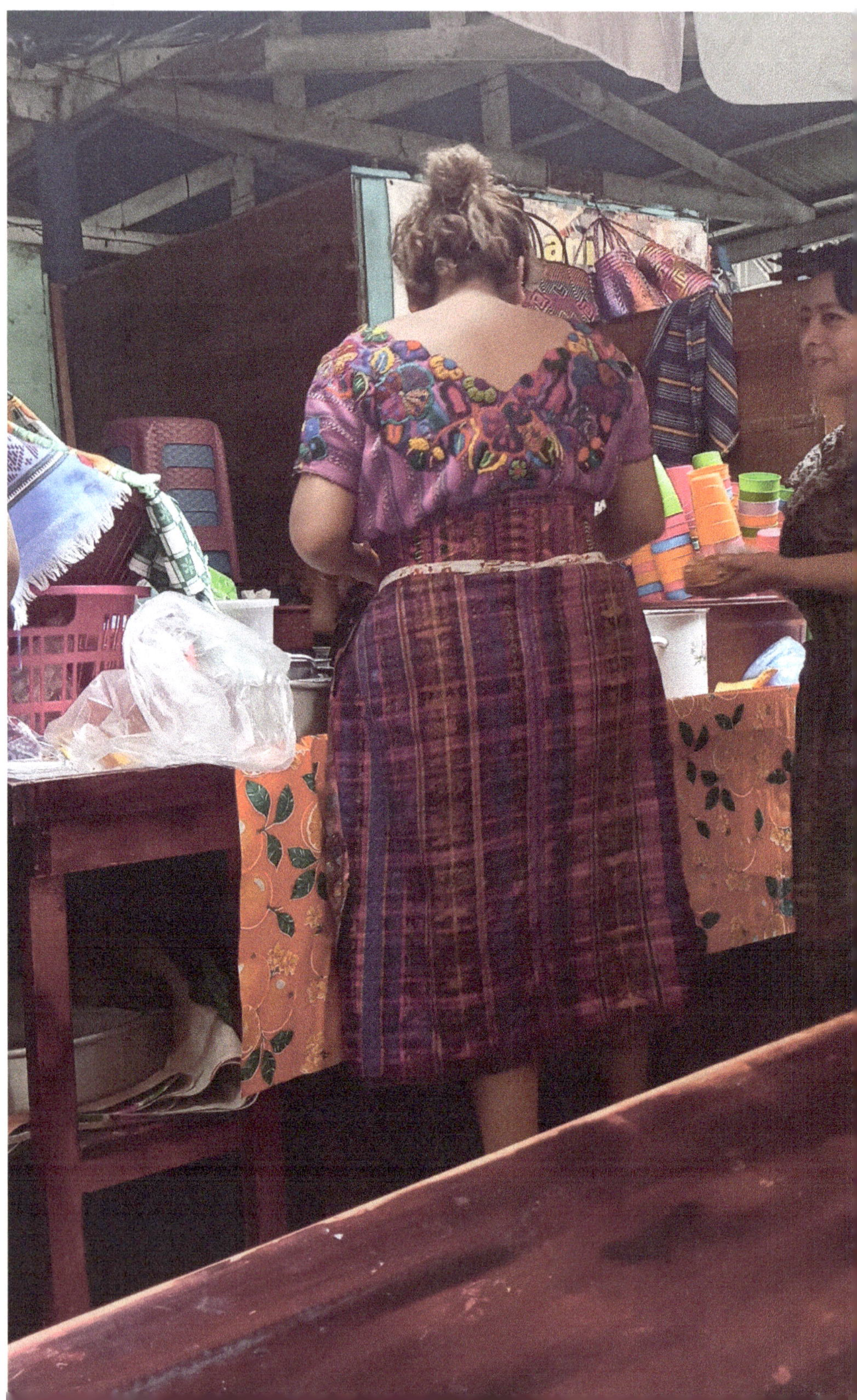

THE MARKET

At the top of the hill is the local market, which goes until about 3pm and has an incredible selection of fresh foods and other local goods.. It's cash only and mostly locals, so be sure to have quetzals & spanish at the ready.

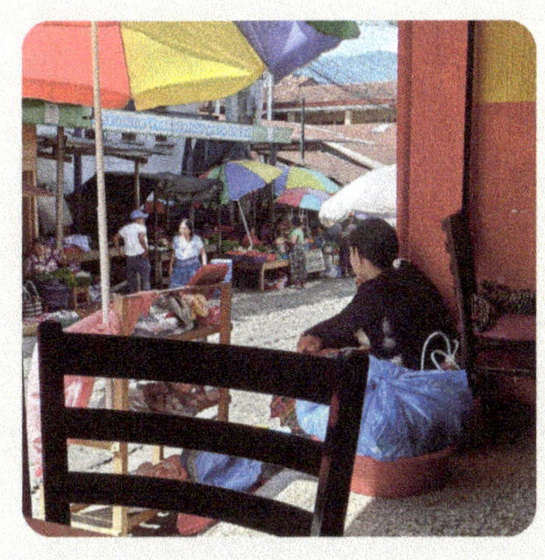

FRUIT STANDS

I loved how they sold fruit here, especially since I was solo for most of the trip. It's cut in slices fresh each day, so you can get just enough for a day or two, and a nice variety for about a dollar.

THE TOSTADAS OF GLORY

At one end of the market is a little food stand, pictured on next page, run by a group of women who are masters of the local cuisine. This is the most authentic food in town, and insanely delicious. At about $1USD per tostada "mixtos", it came with chicken salad, beans, and piles of boiled veggies & eggs. I specifically ate double the day before I left.

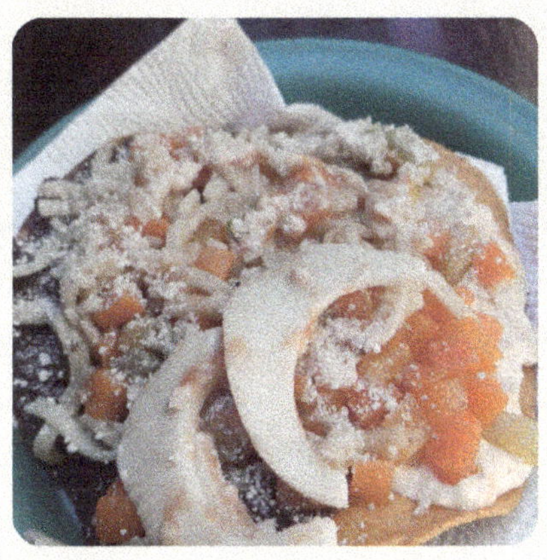

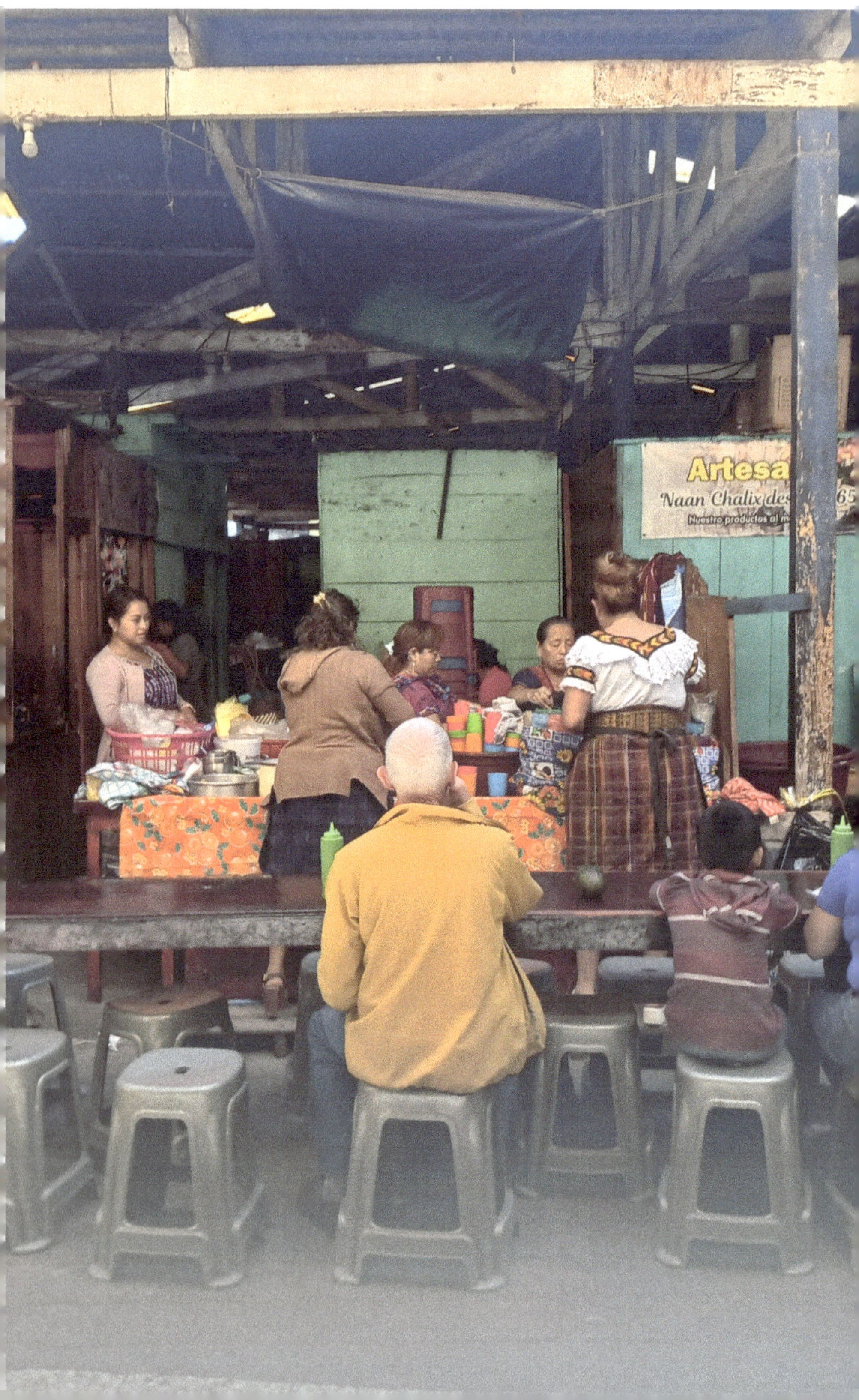
Artesa
Naan Chalix des   65
Nuestro productos al m

THE OVERLOOK CAFE

While avid hikers might be up for the climb, most people should just get a tuktuk to the top of the hill behind the town, then continue the climb to the highest cafe in town. The view is absolutely worth every step!

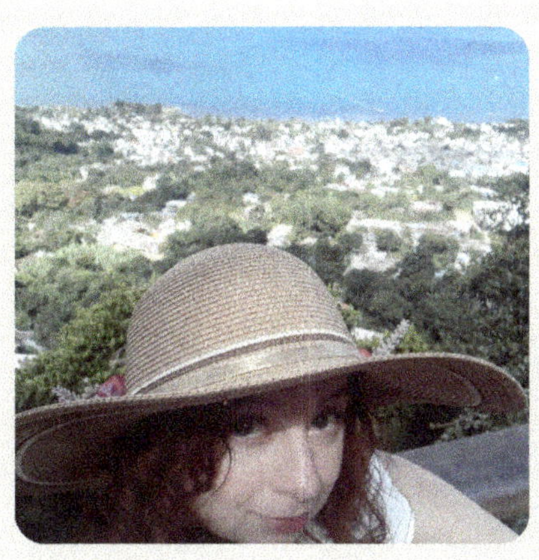

HOT DRINKS

This cafe has a limited menu, mostly drinks, but they are expanding. But really, who cares when you're just there to drink in the sight anyway. More importantly, they have bathrooms, which considering the climb is essential.

HAMMOCK DREAMS

I didn't visit this place often, but the hammocks were a nice touch and wonderful place to relax for the afternoon with a book! There is also a beautiful patio covered in murals for great views and photos.

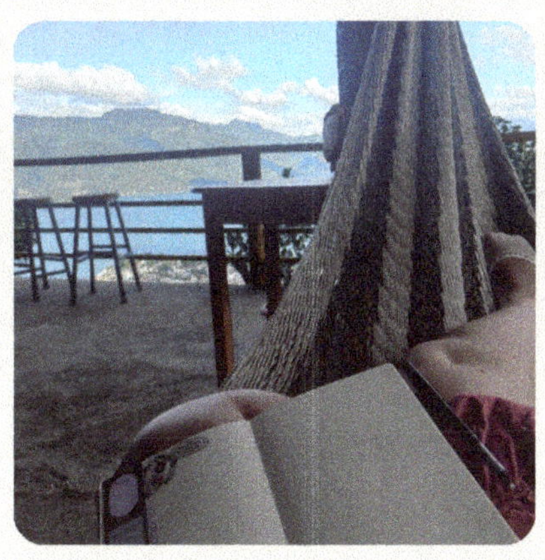

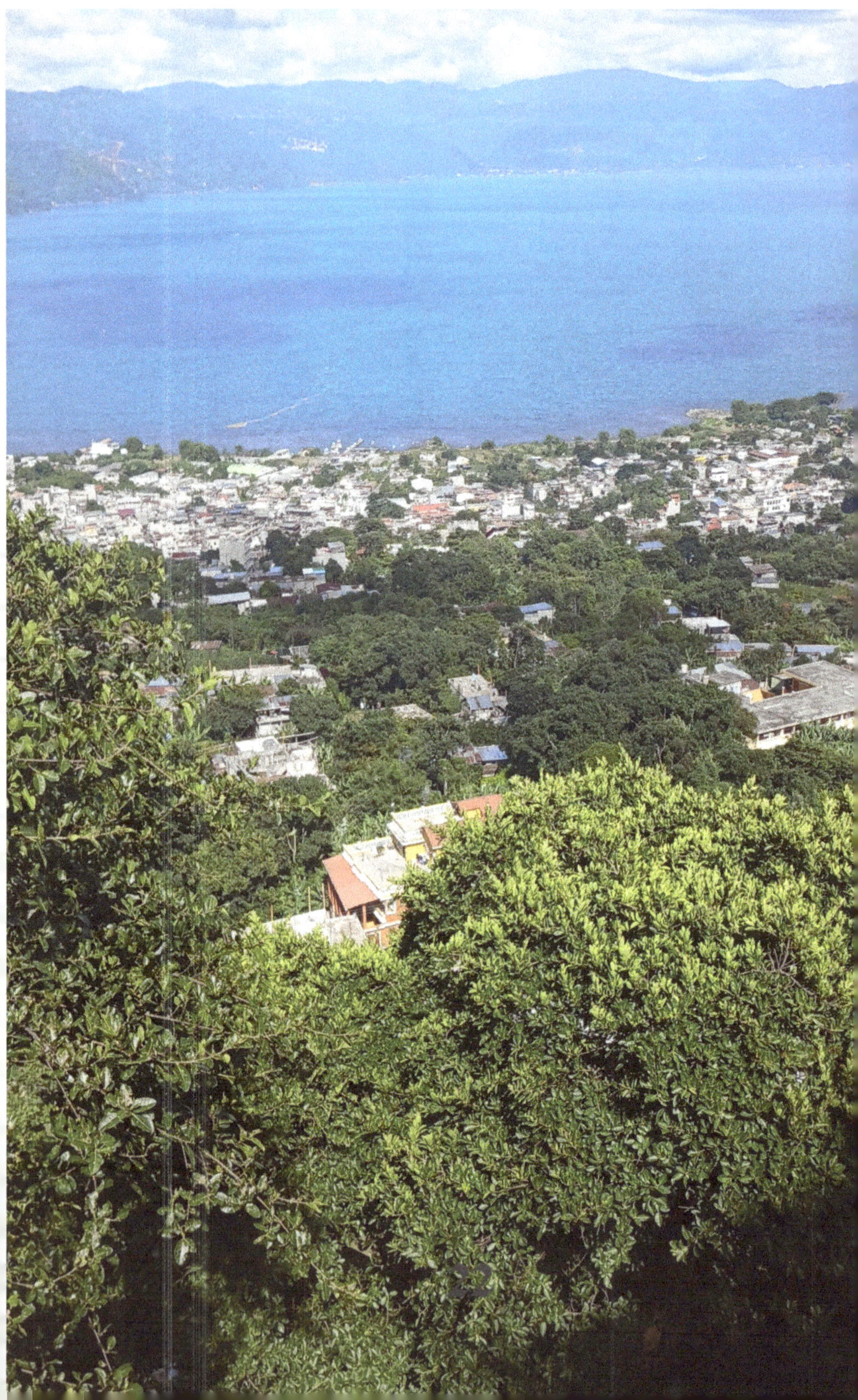

SAN MARCOS

I didn't spend much time in San Marcos, but it has a very impressive food (and party) scene, so here are a couple places worth mentioning.

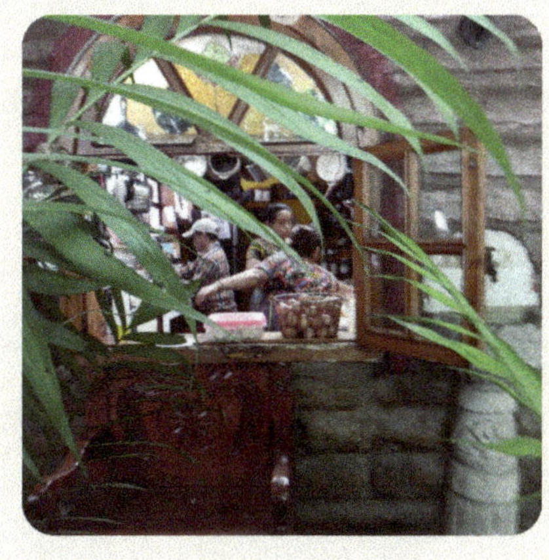

IL GARDINO

With a lovely garden vibe and friendly cats, this is also one of the few places in San Marcos that serves meat. The cacao is not the best, but the juice is amazing and the food healthy, filling, and delicious.

COMEDOR KONOJEL

Pictured right is something called a "pupusa", this one with chicken, and it's an iconic local dish. This restaurant in particular was featured in Lonely Planet because truly, it's worth going all the way into the jungle just to taste this deliciousness. Avocado, veggies, shredded spiced chicken & friend dough, what else could be better?

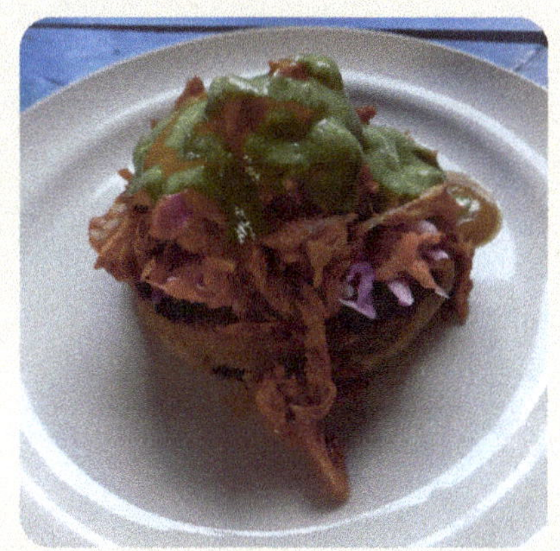

2019

COMEDOR KONOJEL

Text

LISTED AS A TOP CHOICE BY

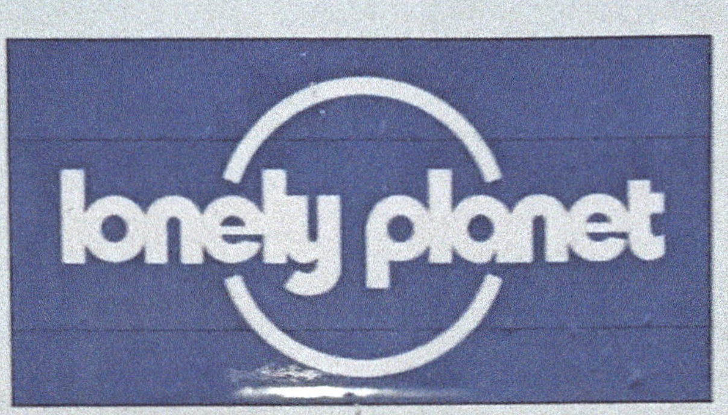

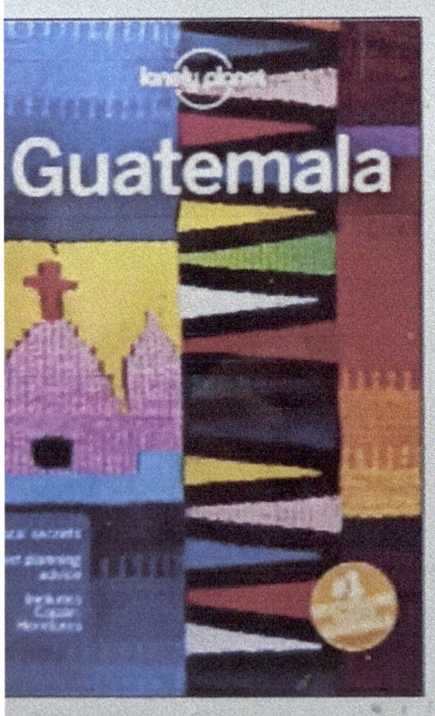

✕ Eating

★ **Comedor Konojel** GUATEMALAN
(daily specials Q30) This cheerily-painted clapboard canteen serves up big healthy portions
of Guatemalan food according to a changing
daily menu to help support a wider feeding
program and other community projects in
the area around San Marcos. Doing good
rarely tastes so delicious.

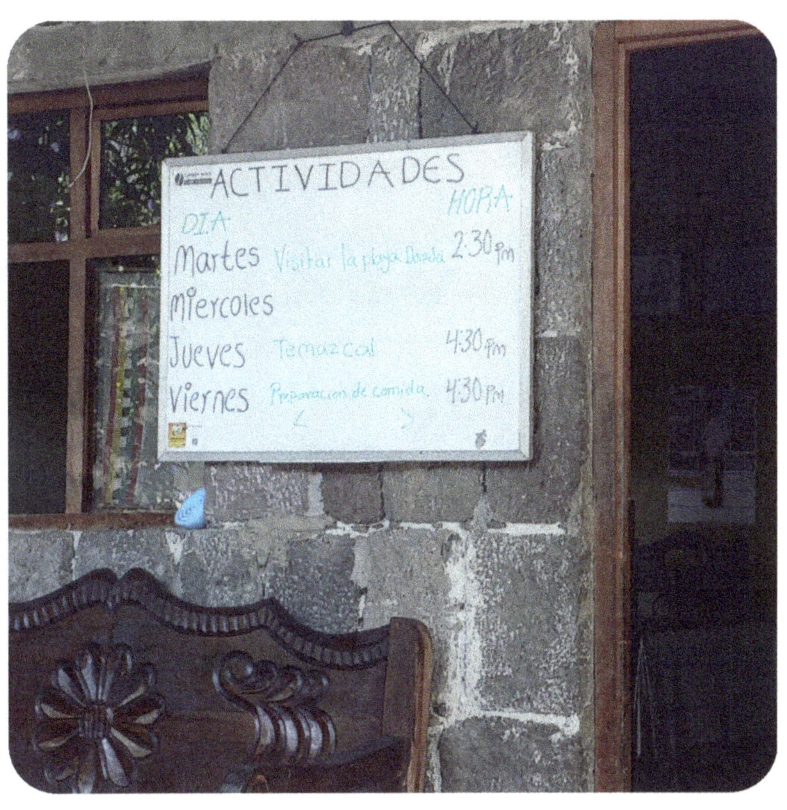

OTHER ACTIVITIES

While my time was spent primarily working on my books and enjoying cafes, San Pedro does have a number of other activities to offer. It's particularly well known for its Spanish Language and Mayan cooking schools, and for chocolate making classes. The local people have done an incredible job of preserving their culture by becoming teachers of their own traditions.

A BIT OF CULTURE

- The Pre-Christian traditions were much more matriarchal and had a lot of influence of "4's"- four colors, four directions, the four Godmothers (the Goddesses of the Lake"), all corresponding to one another. While Catholicism is predominant today, they still practice a lot of the old traditions (holy days, respect for the Lake, etc.) and hold women in respect.

- One of the forms of respect is in the men providing for the women. It's very common for most of the local people, especially the women, to wear the traditional garments of beautifully embroidered shirts & woven wool skirts. They are very expensive, even by American standards, and a man is not allowed to marry a woman unless he can provide her with these clothes. The variety a woman has is a mark of wealth and status for the man & the family.

- I heard a lot of stories about a 'Spirit of the Volcano' who lives in & around the lake. I'm not certain how accurate any of what I heard is, because it was told to me by ex-pats, not native peoples. Nevertheless, it did seem based in some old stories, and there was definitely a lot of ritual & spiritual practices based on respect for the Lake, and the Volcanos that surround it.

- The casual artistry of the people is truly incredible. There is a lot of skill in handicrafts of various kinds, especially fabrics & beadwork, or anything to do with weaving really. I saw gorgeous pottery and woodworks as well, and the paintings were incredible. As a painter myself, I spent a lot of time admiring the murals on every street and the impressive level of detail in all of them, (Mexico has a lot too, but they are more simplified in design.) The woven bag I got at the market, and the wood-carved & painted journal I got for my husband, are some of our favorite, and most beautiful, items in our home. I would definitely recommend some extra money and suitcase space for the impressive collection of goods available.

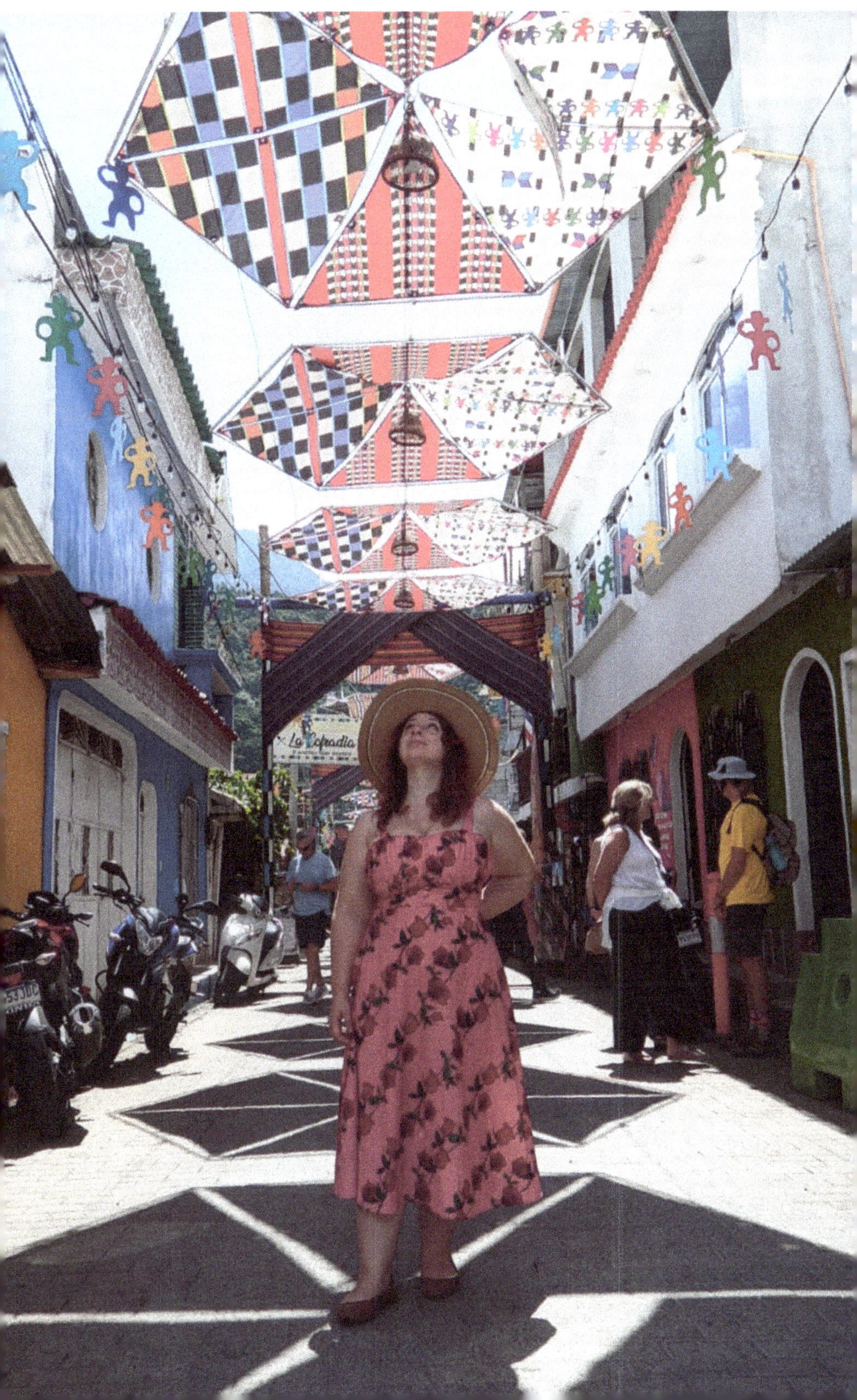

LOCAL MUSEUM

There is a lovely little museum with the history of the area, along with displays of local art, artifacts, and photos. There is a little video documentary to watch and a section about local geography as well.
Note: It is all in Spanish and they do not allow photos.

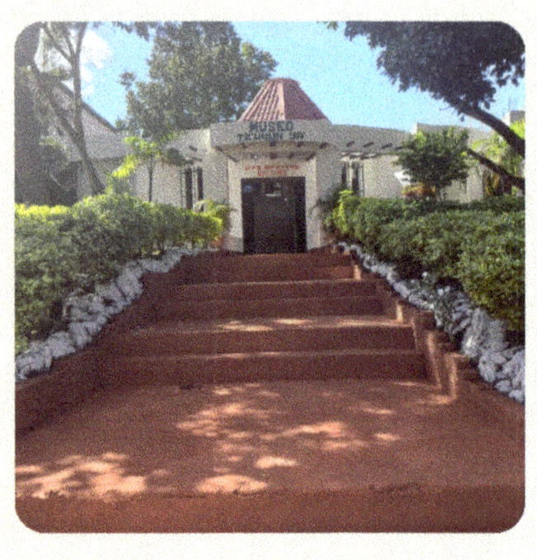

HIKING & KAYAKING

Hiking is inevitable in this region, just walking down the street is good exercise in a town built on a hillside, but there's lots of trails all around town as well. Renting boats & kayaks is also a regular activity.

TOWN EVENTS

There were multiple parades and festivals while I was there, and quite a few locations have various live music, karaoke, and other events on a near nightly basis.

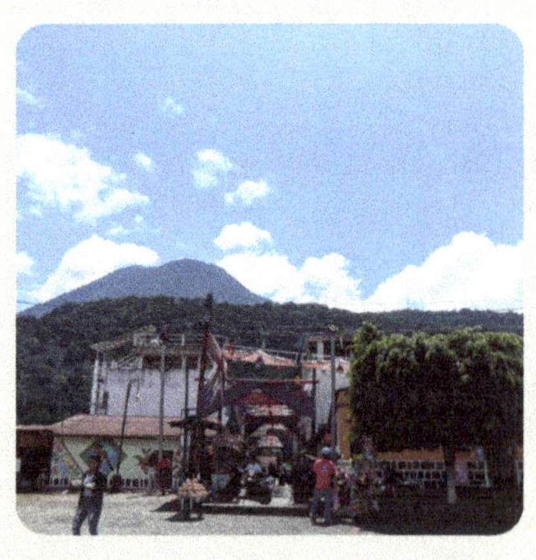

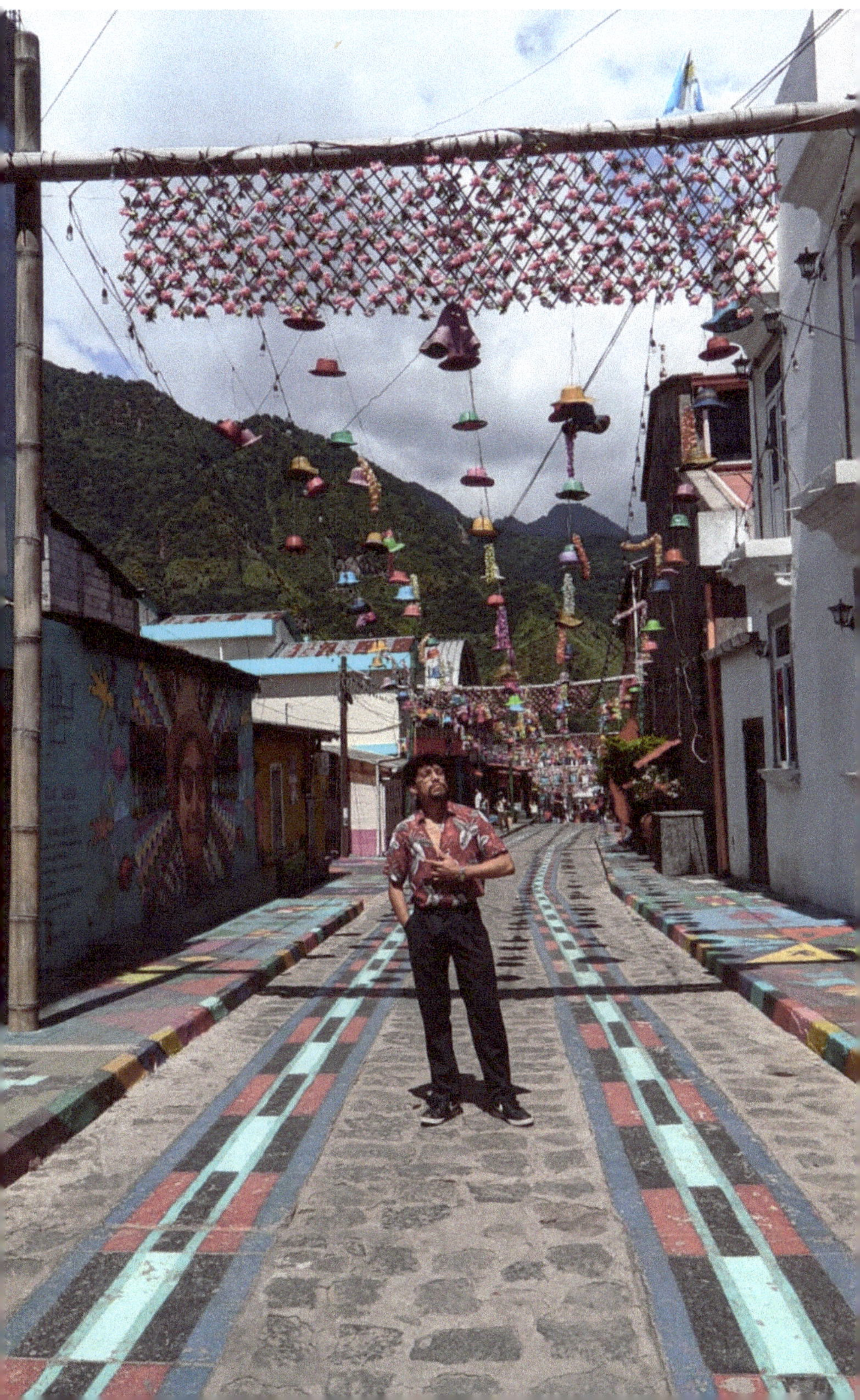

4
FOR THE LOVE OF HONEY
& CACAO

MUNDO DE ABEJAS MAYAS
THE MAYAN BEE SANCTUARY

While San Pedro is the best for quiet daily life, and San Marcos for Tourist activities, San Juan La Laguna is the place for cultural activities and events. Specifically tours for Honey & Chocolate, one of the main reasons I was looking to visit the area overall.

The Mayan Bee Sanctuary is on the edge of the village, since it's a massive garden with coffee & chocolate trees, roses, and pathways through plantings of the Three Sisters and other native agricultural techniques. They offer detailed and informative tours for a minimal fee, and includes samples of the products. Everything is owned and maintained by the local Mayan people & the proceeds go to preserve the local plants, and of course, the Bees.

There is, of course, a little Shop where I got my honey with bee pollen for my morning tea, along with honey beer, and honey filled chocolates.

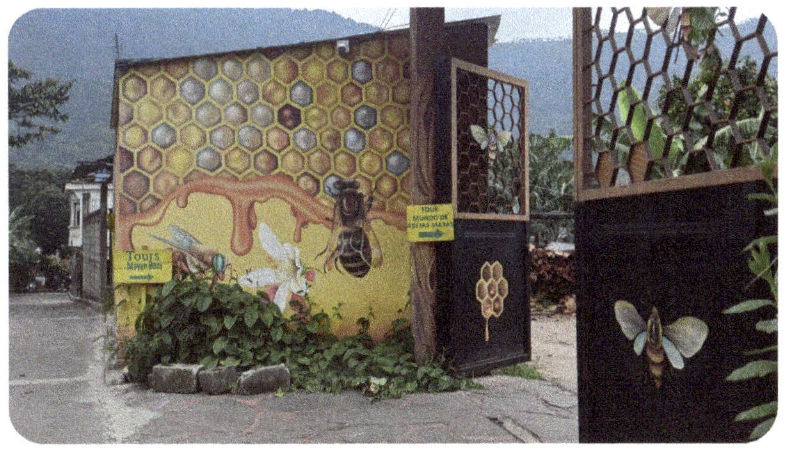

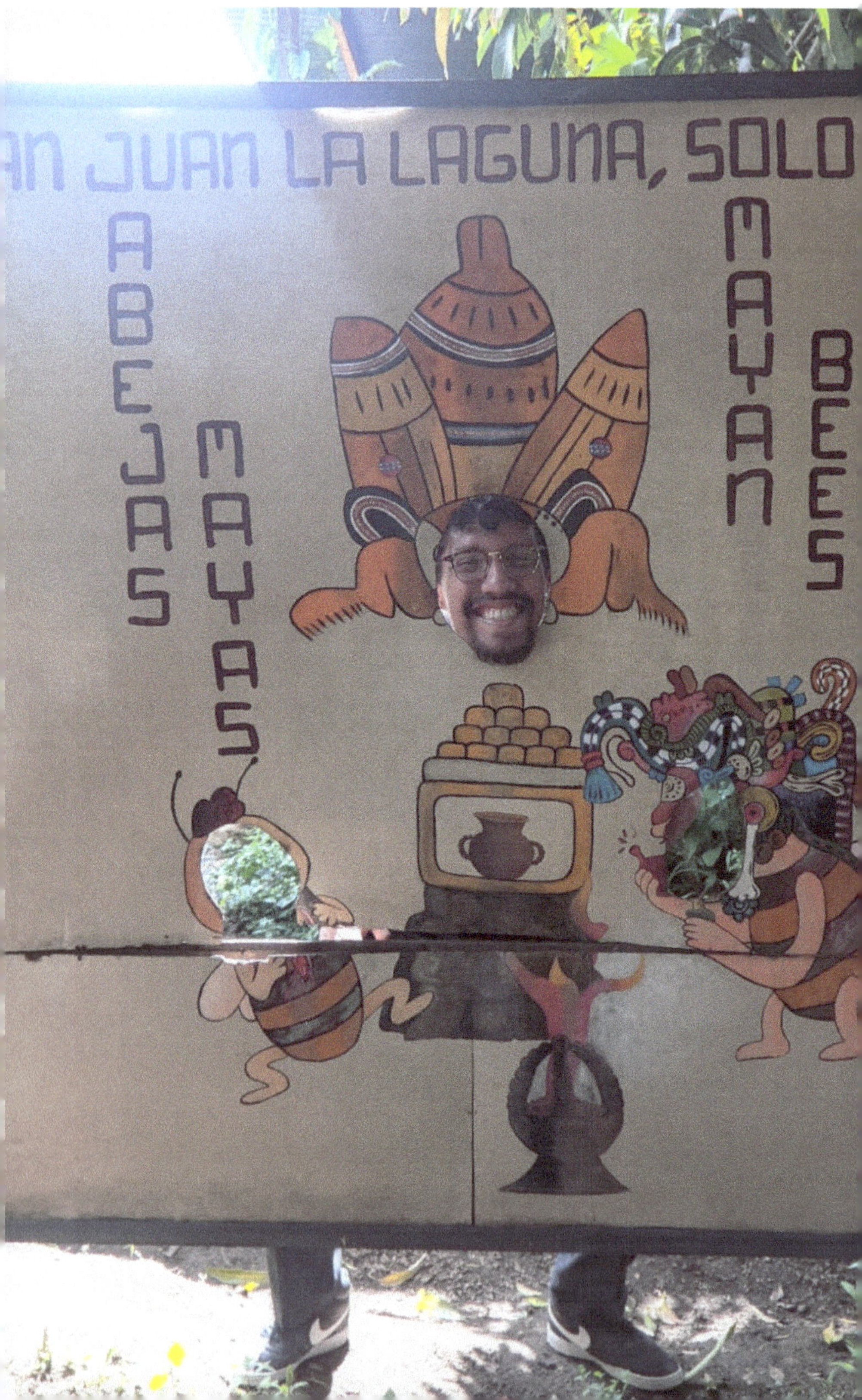
AN JUAN LA LAGUNA, SOLO
ABEJAS
MAYAS
MAYAN
BEES

VIEW FROM THE CAFE

The Bee Sanctuary also has a lovely cafe above the shop with coffee made from their own gardens. The view of the garden is a relaxing place to find some creative inspiration as well.

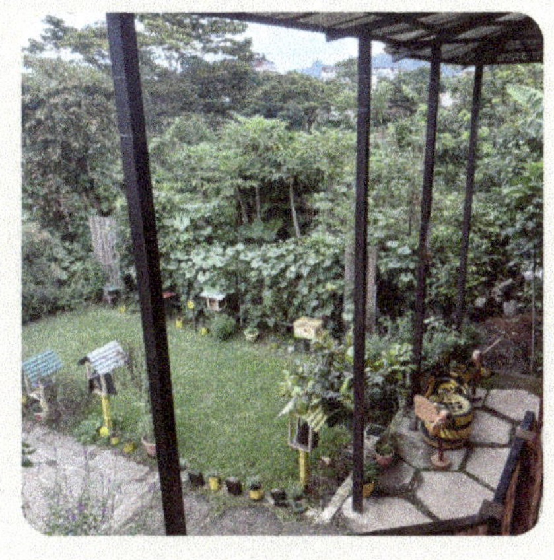

HONEY TREATS

I used the honey with bee pollen from this place my whole time in the area. But I particularly loved the chocolate made with honey I found here. They have a lovely shop with all kinds of food & beauty items made in house with their incredible honey.

GARDEN DELIGHTS

There are multiple different garden areas in this compound and it was amazing to see coffee, chocolate, and other local plants in full production, along with the traditional gardening methods, such as the 'Three Sisters' plantings.

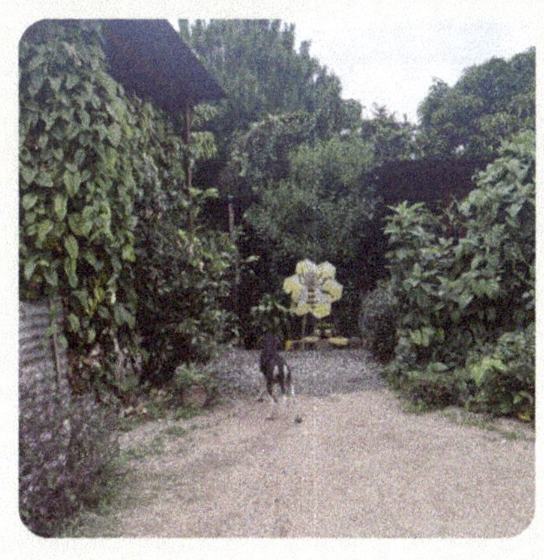

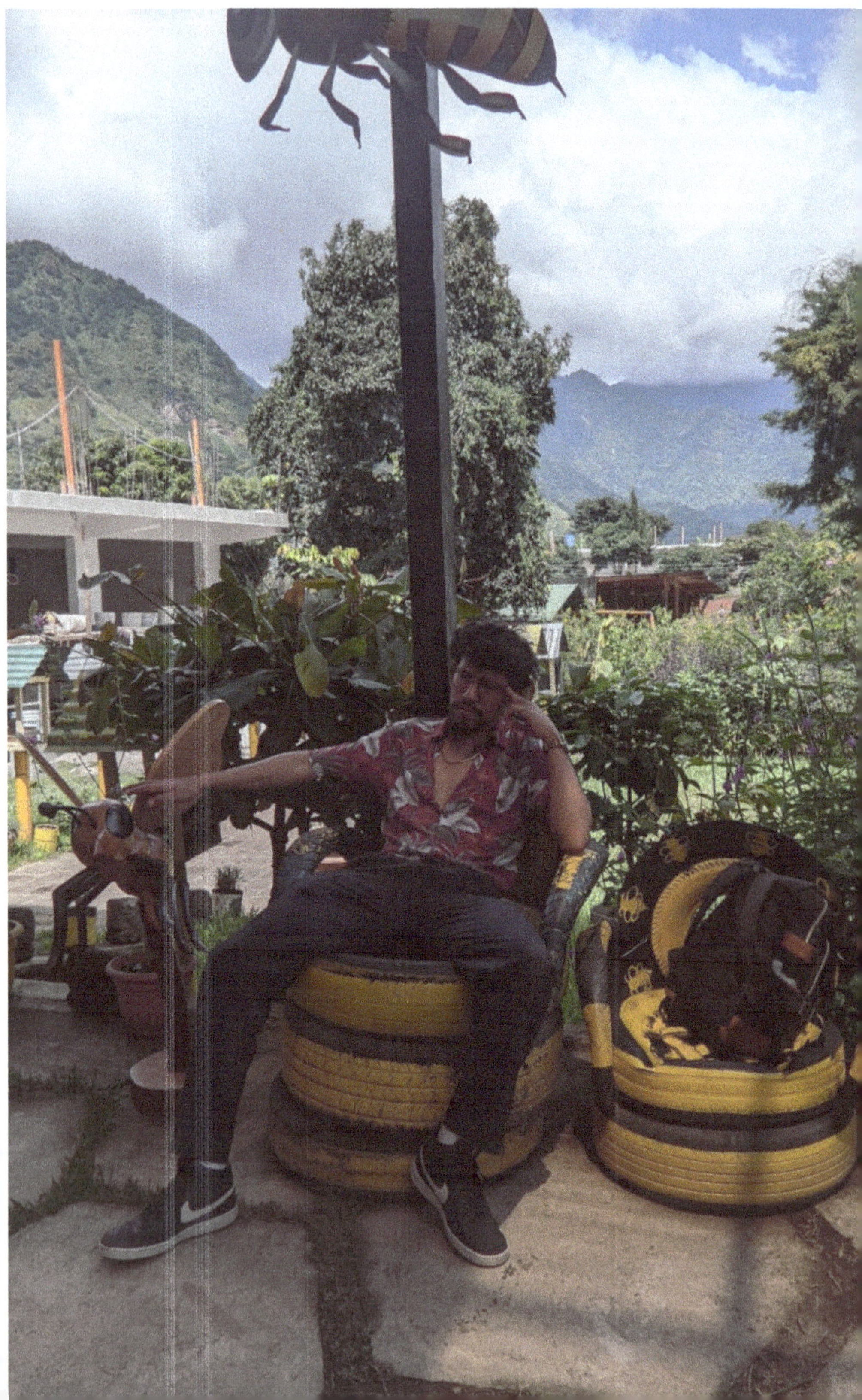

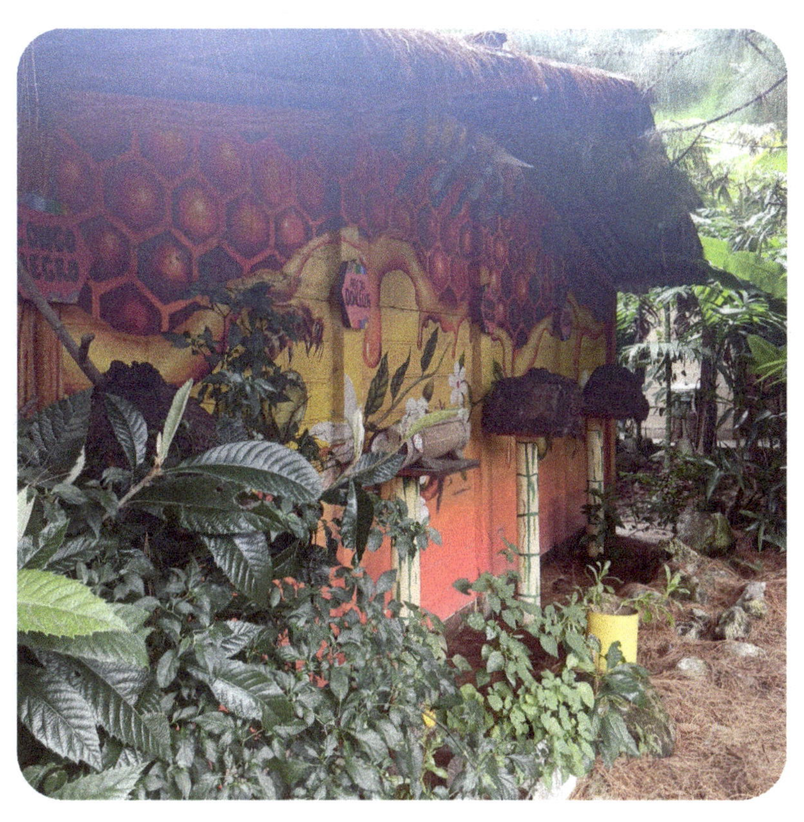

ALL THE BEES!

The Sanctuary also has a little "bee garden" with hives of each of the 1w native Bees they protect. It's perfectly safe to walk through, slowly, very slowly, and watch the little bees do their dances. While I've worked with honeybees before, it was incredible to see the wide variety of sizes and colors that exist in the area.
I absolutely adore how dedicated the people are to preserving their traditions & lands, and believe anyone who goes to the are should do what they can to support this impressive program.

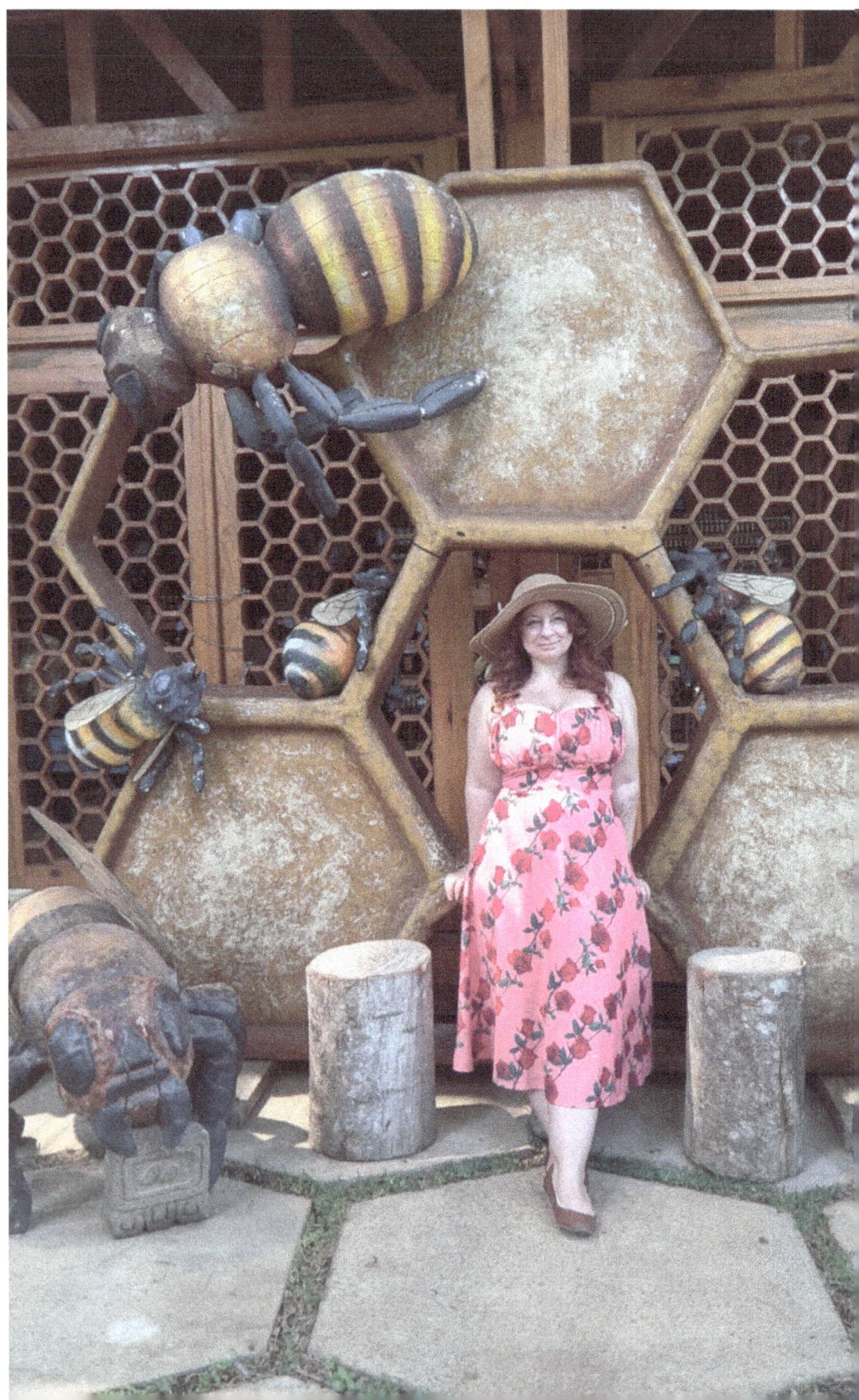

LICOR MARRON CHOCOLATE

This little hotel & restaurant also offers chocolate making classes and has a shop full of local chocolate candies. But I recommend the café, the upper levels are set in the literal treetops, and the hot chocolate is truly divine. Currently it ranks #3 of all the chocolate I've had in my life.

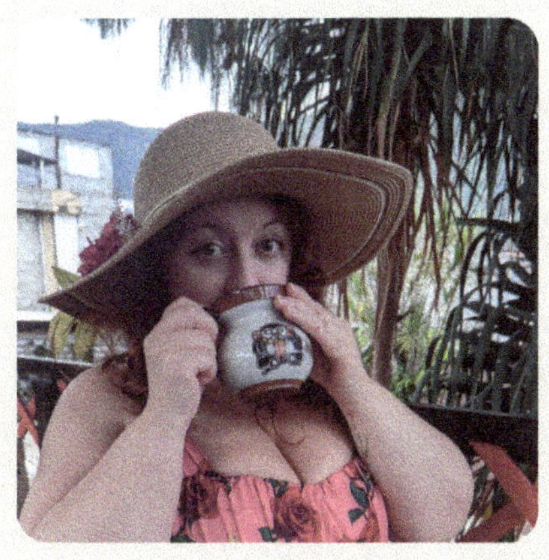

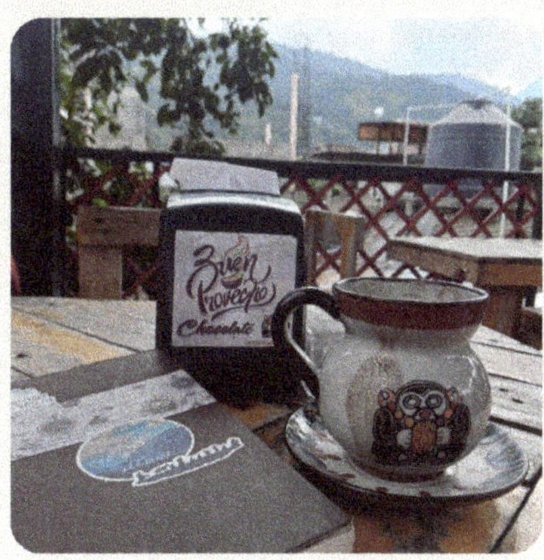

TREETOP WORLD

This location is also perfect for anyone into birdwatching, I saw half a dozen differnt species nesting and playing in the trees around just the cafe platform.

GUATEMALAN CHOCOLATE

There are quite a few other places that sell variations of the local style, which mixes orange juice instead of milk, and is a soft paste rather than a hard bar. It's mixed in various ways, but I favored the berry or honey mixes for sure.

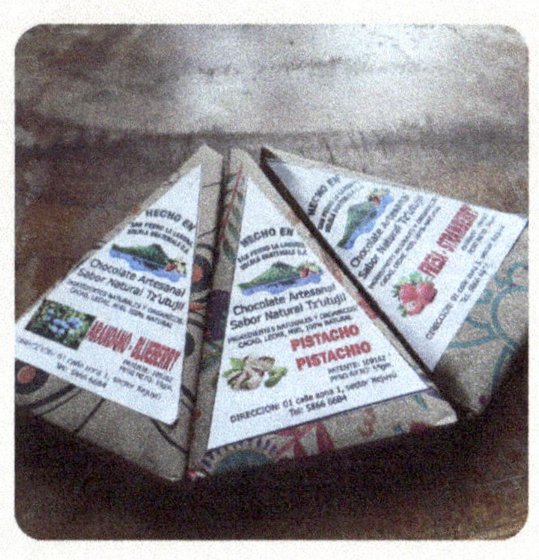

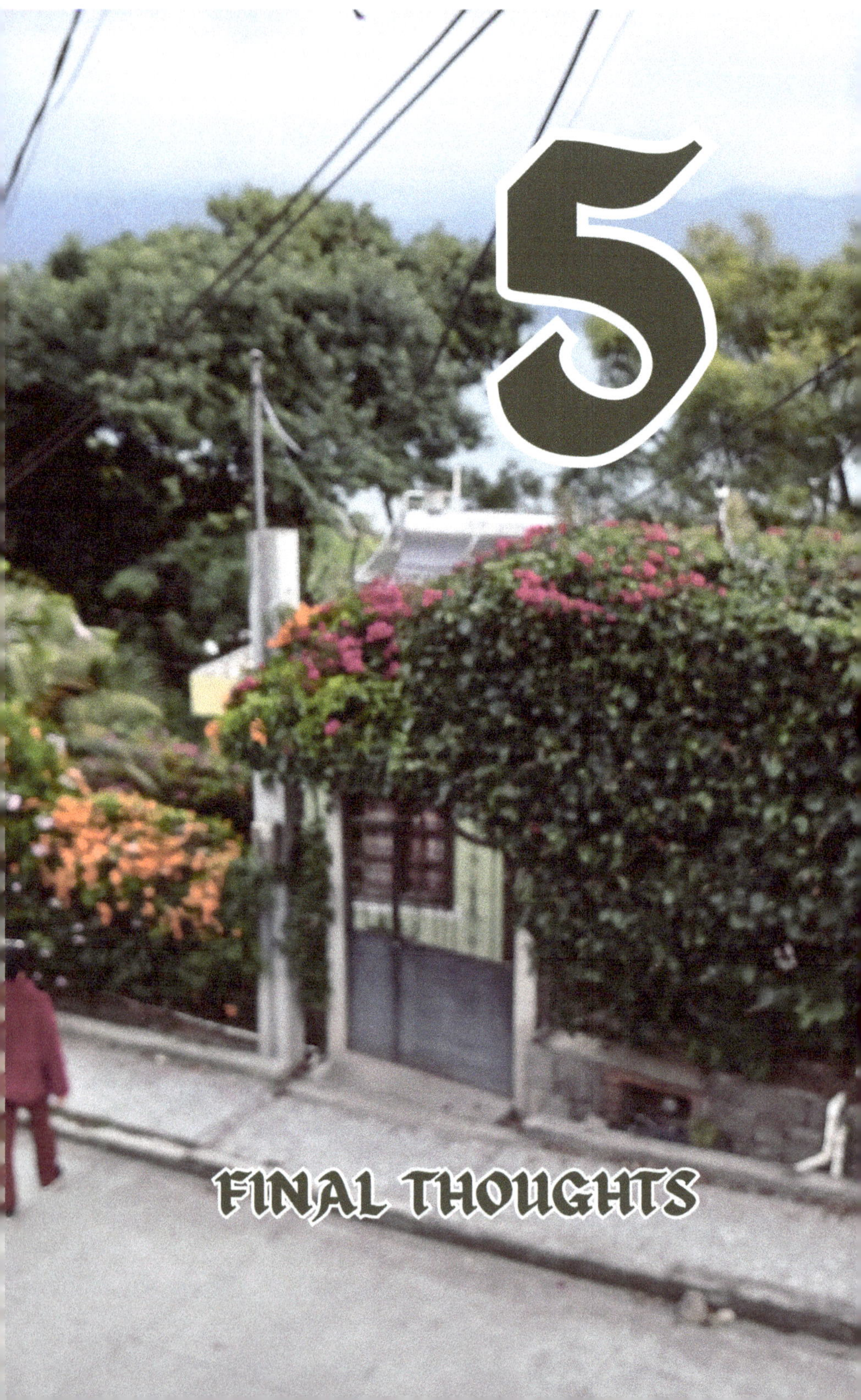
5
FINAL THOUGHTS

A PLACE OF BEAUTY & SURVIVAL

I believe it would be difficult, and wrong of me, to write about Guatemala without acknowledging the impact colonization has had on the culture. In full disclosure, I considered not writing this book at all, because I didn't want to add to the tourism culture developing in the area. But I hope that by writing this, and including some awareness of these issues, my readers may be more respectful to the people and better enjoy their experience in the region.

Due to its location, affordability, beautiful natural wonders, and bus routes, Guatemala is a popular destination for backpackers and let's just say Hippie vibes (keeping in mind I'm quite the Hippie myself). On the good side, this leads to things like the excellent health-food store, and appreciation and maintenance of the nature in the area.

 Downsides included people being naked in public & in the Lake, doing vast amounts of drugs, and generally spiritually appropriating a lot of the local culture. While technically all legal, it was much to the horror of the local people who, even pre-Christian, were a very modest & more conservative culture.

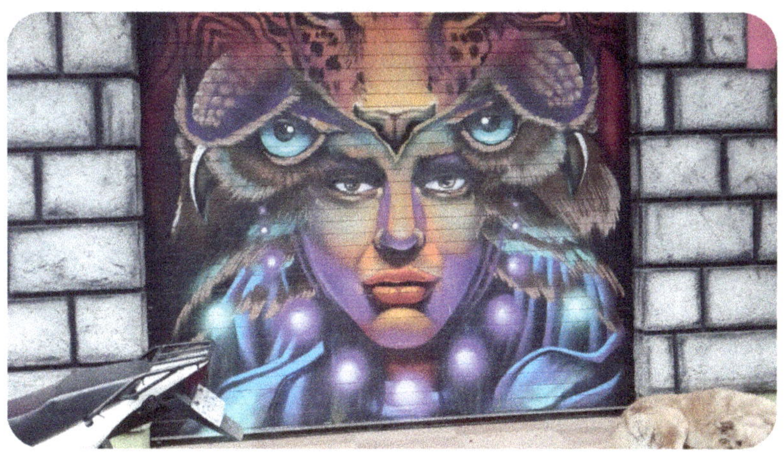

I was also quite concerned at the number of people from other countries who claimed to love Guatemala, had spent extended time there, were seeking or had residency visas & property, yet spoke very little Spanish, if any (even after decades), and had no close relationships with local people at the Lake.
(A few mentioned friends from other parts of Guatemala, but none from the local lake tribes.)

Of the few I met who were fluent and had local connections, the relationship seemed, while affectionate, primarily based on business needs (long-term renters, managing property, handling legal issues, or shipping products). Overall, it felt like experiencing parallel worlds co-existing, "local" & "other" in a way that was surreal compared to my other travel experiences.

The truth is, I felt very strongly that the local people would be perfectly fine, if not happier, if a foreigner never showed up again. It wasn't dangerous per se, they were generally polite, but I was definitely severely overcharged, occasionally outright scammed, lied to, or taken advantage of at great frequency until I learned the system much better. It might seem naïve, but it was not an issue I'd experienced in other countries such as Mexico, Moldova, Italy, etc, especially not to the near constant extent.

None of this is a complaint; with the amount of disrespect I saw towards their home, I can understand why they may consider it a reasonable extra tax on the tourists that so widely impact their lives. And I did notice that after my (now) husband, who is Mexican, came to visit and spoke with a number of them on our little adventures, the interactions were much more friendly for the rest of my stay.

I write all of this simply as a warning, and a commentary: while it is a wonderful place to visit, please, be courteous to the local community as much as possible. They have done a truly incredible job in preserving their traditions, and they deserve respect in their home, and in their country.

A FEW EXTRA TIPS:

- While it is a tropical climate, the mountain jungle is different from the coastal areas and get quite chilly, especially at night. Long sleeves, layers for different times of day (warm afternoons, cold nights/mornings), and light jackets are recommended.

- There is no public (cheap) shuttle to anywhere at Lake Atitlan from the airport after 8 am. Nor do many of the flights, if any at all, arriving get there before 8 am. So, you'll either need to stay in Guatemala City until the next day, or pay for a private shuttle directly to the Lake (about $100-150). However, it is more comfortable and quick.

- Get a local SIM card at the airport ($15) and save yourself a lot of trouble. You can get the data recharged at a number of little convenience stores all over any of the towns.

- The best purchase I think I've ever made in my life was one of the woven bags from the market. All of the local women were using them, so I picked one up for about $10 USD, and I'm quite certain it would be a primary survival item in the apocalypse. It's reasonably nice looking and can hold a week's worth of food for two people, and a whole watermelon. It's irrational how much it holds. The limit is *your* strength, not the bag's.

- There are really good clothing and thrift stores around the lake, don't overpack, you'll definitely want to pick stuff up there.

- San Pedro in particular is known for its schools, there are quite a few language, cooking, and dance schools in the area, which are great places to meet people, if like me, you're not a bar 'n drinks type person.

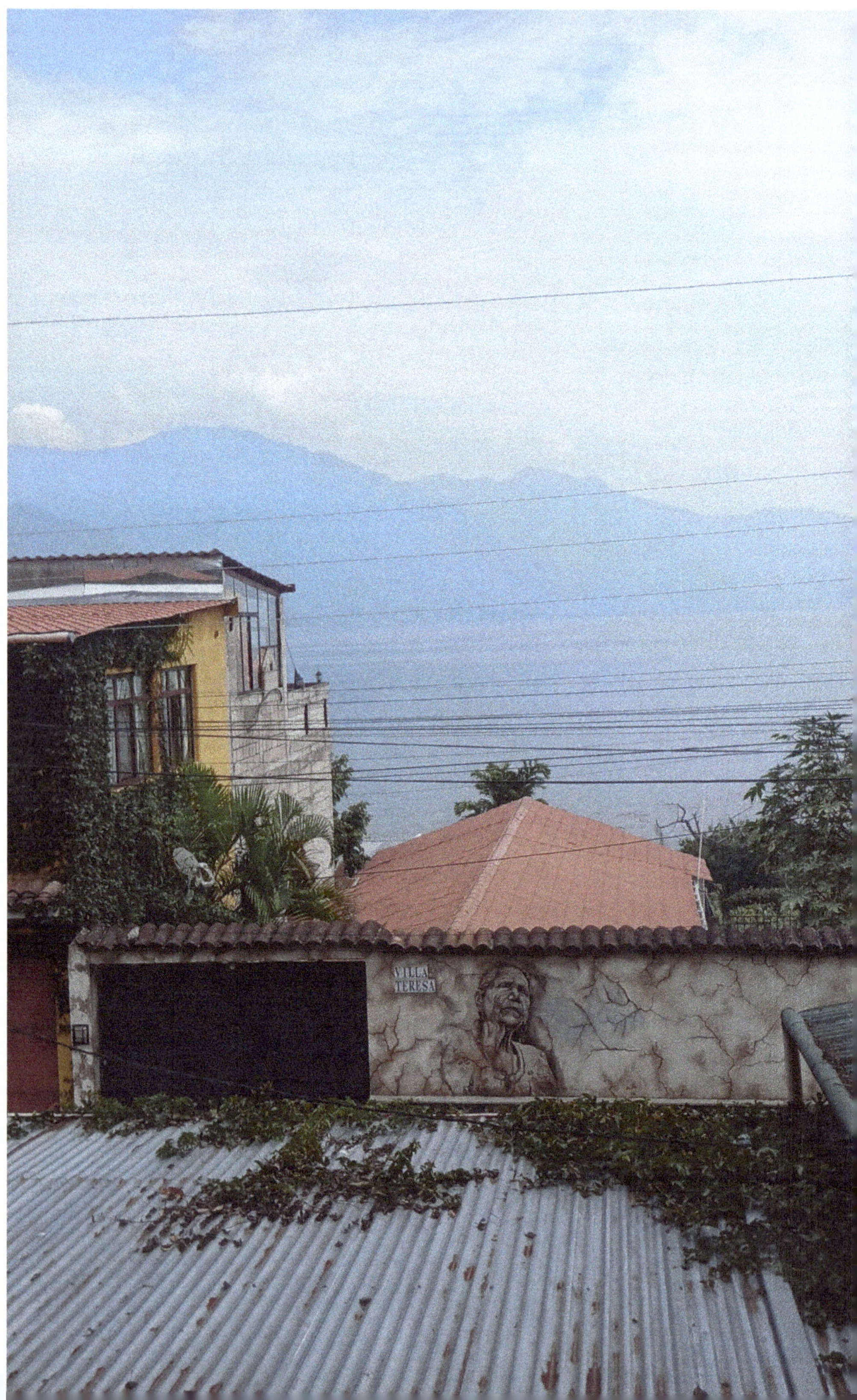

VILLA
TERESA

PHOTO GALLERY

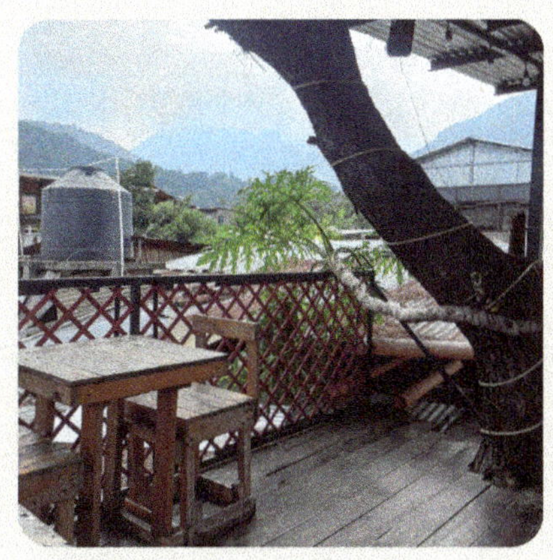

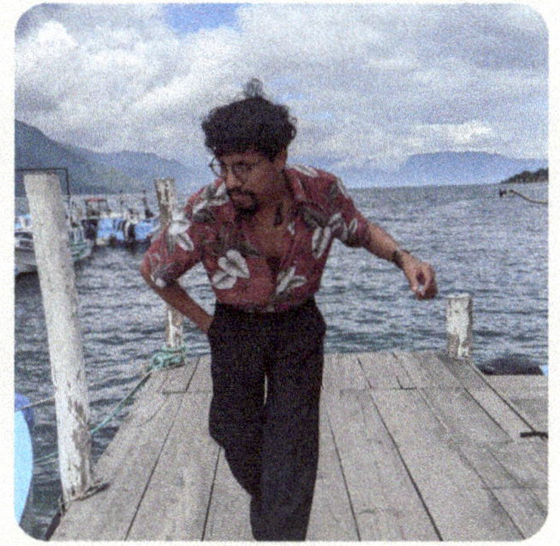

LAKE DANCING

Dr. Pierce enjoying some music on the pier.

Kamui used to be the only sushi spot in San Pedro, but it has since closed, so now we are simply left with pictures and appreciation that I got to enjoy it while I was there.

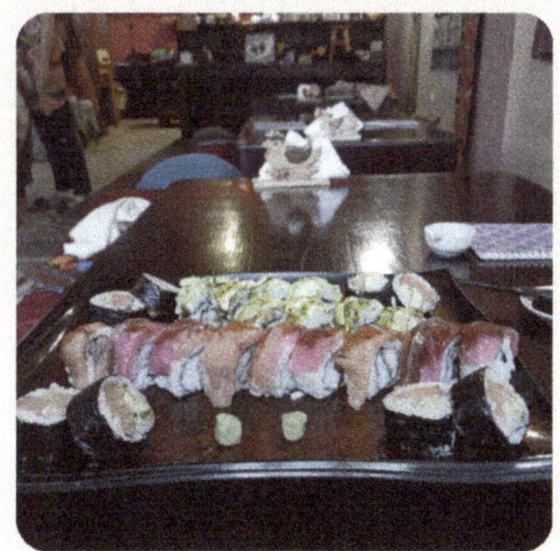

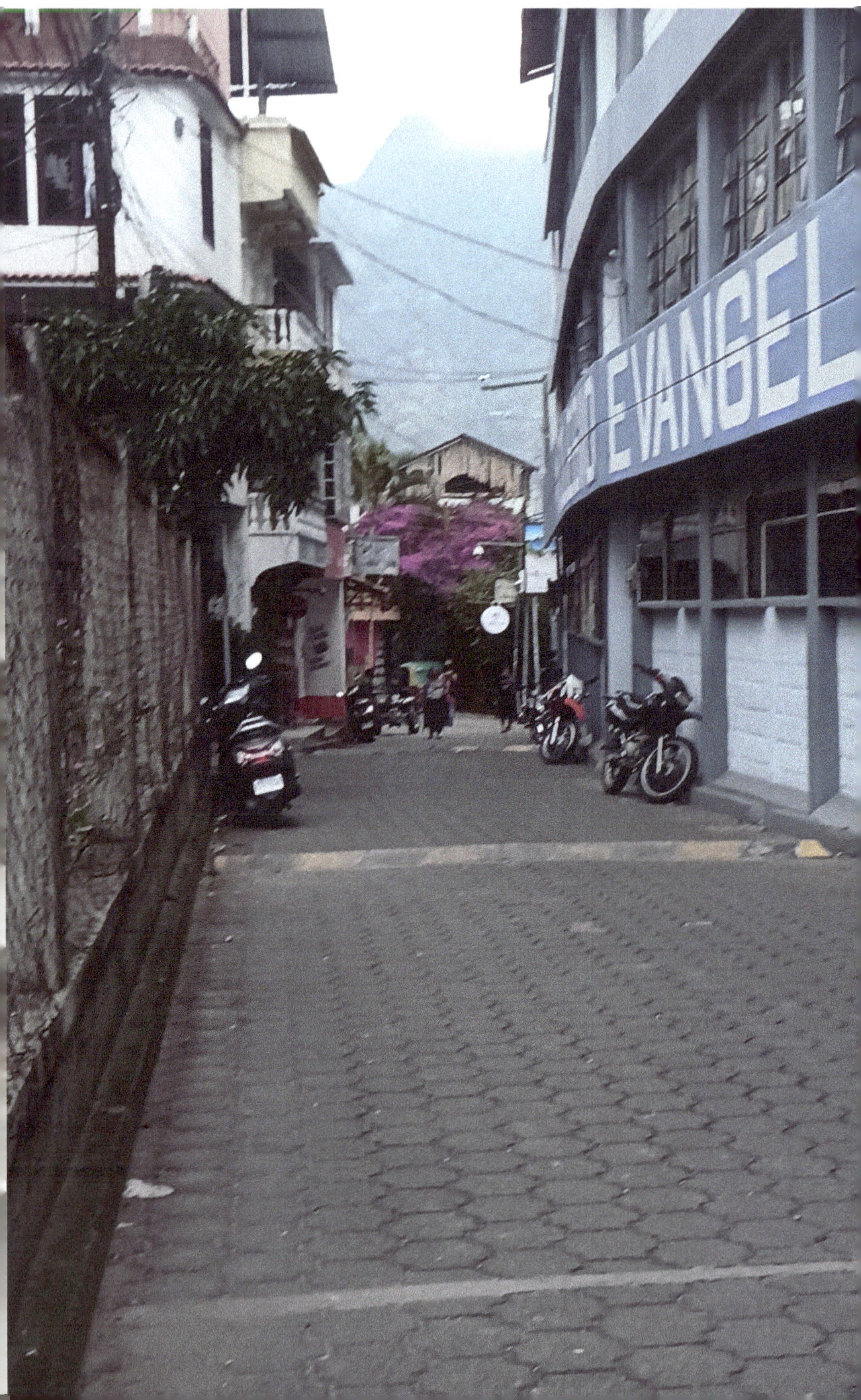
EVANGEL

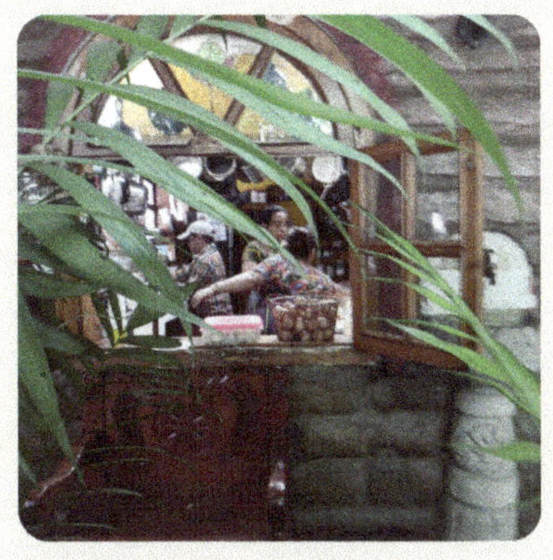
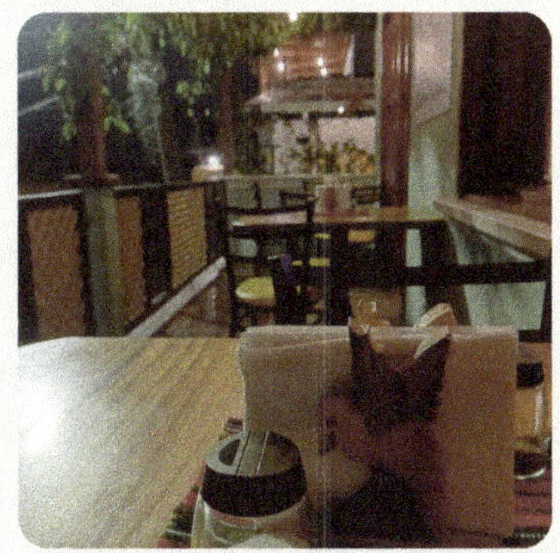
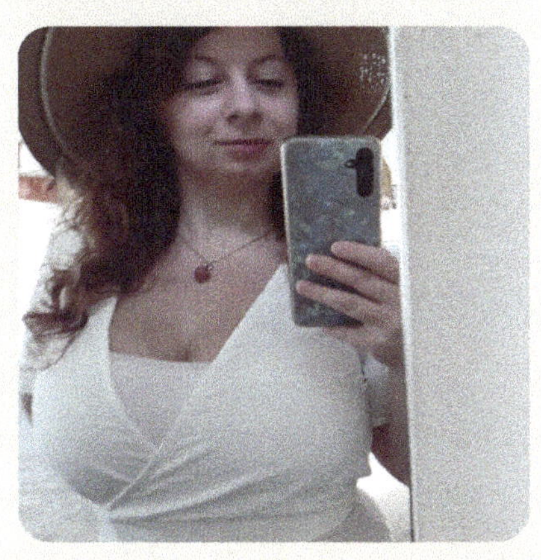
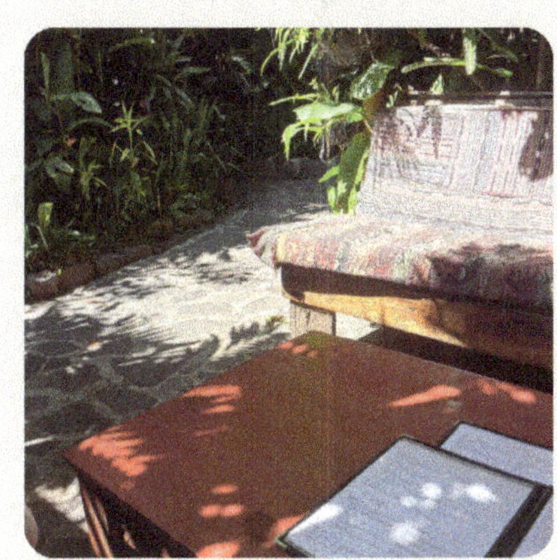
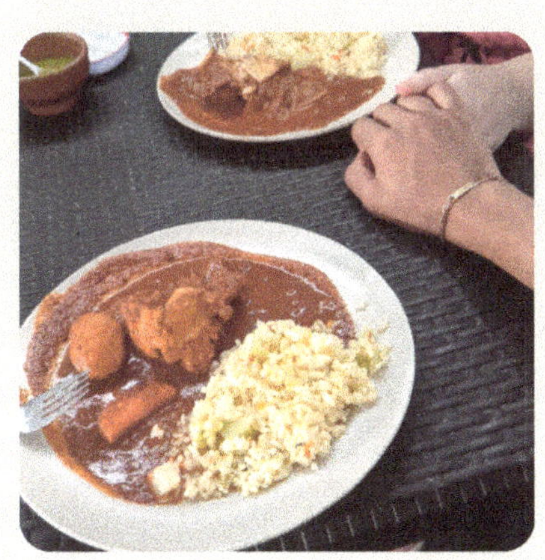
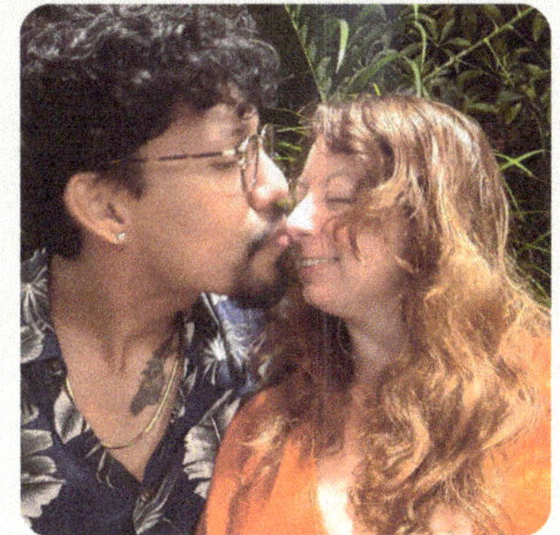

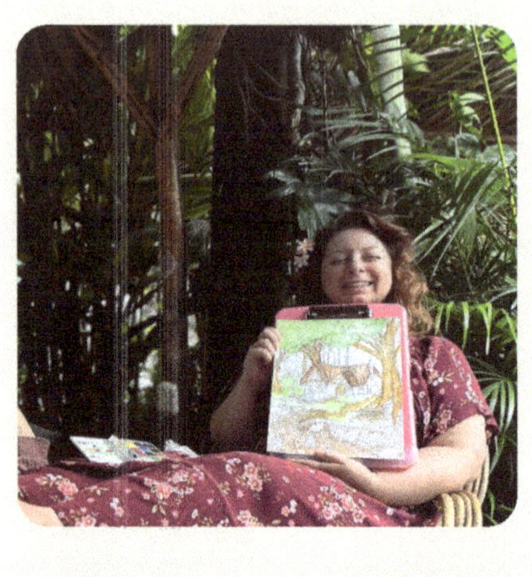
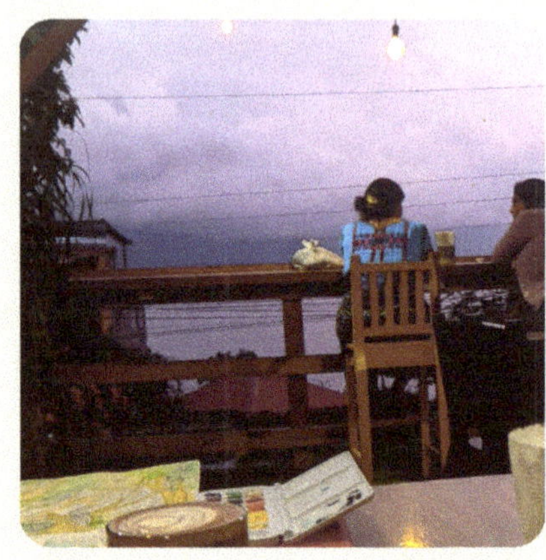
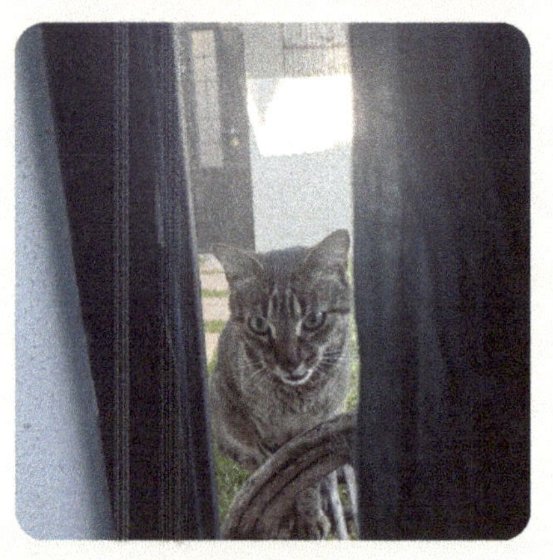
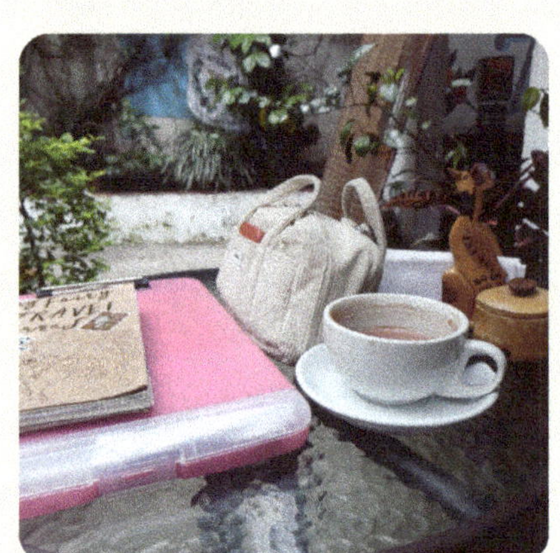
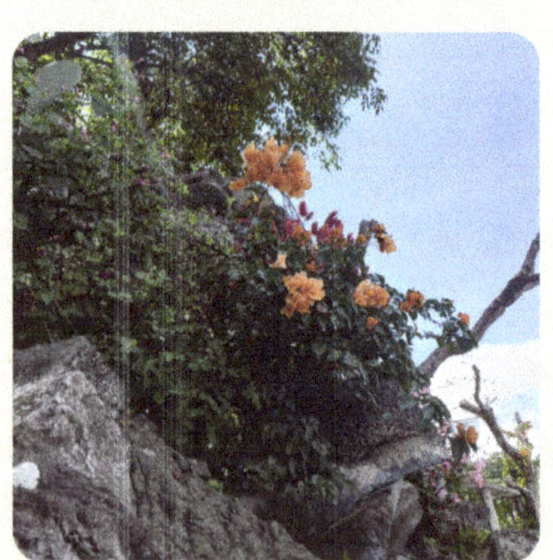
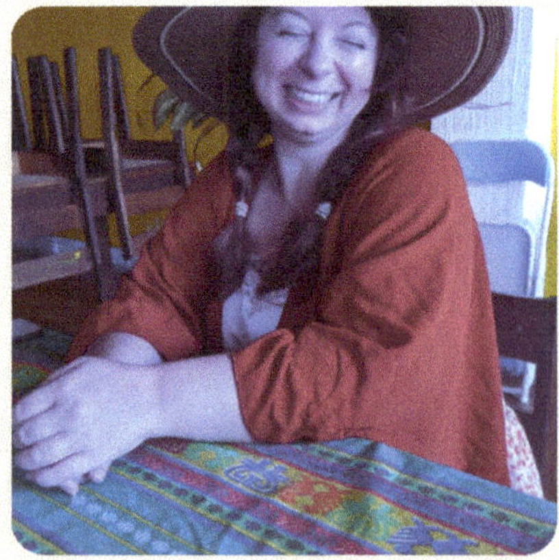

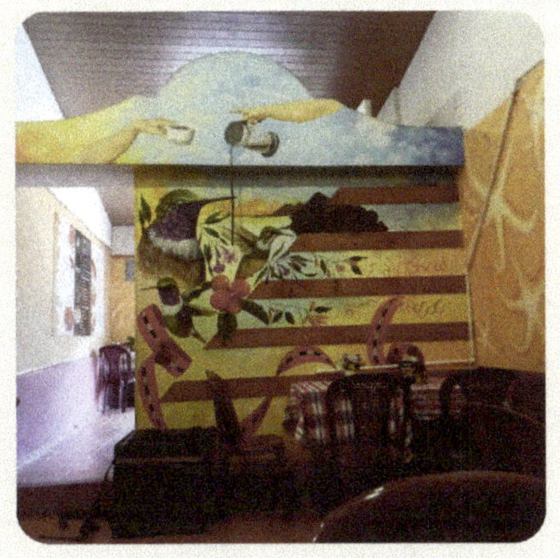

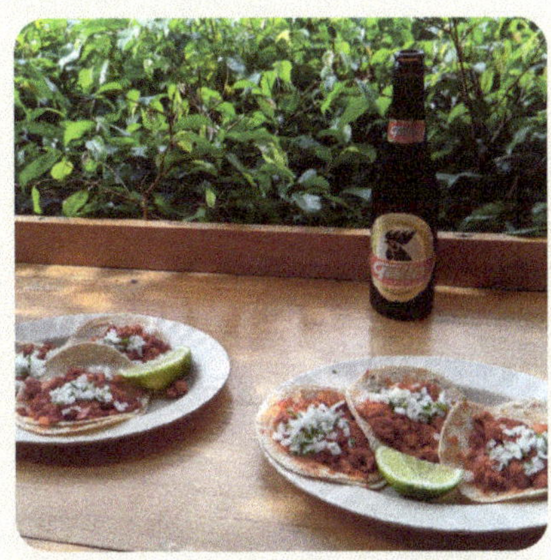

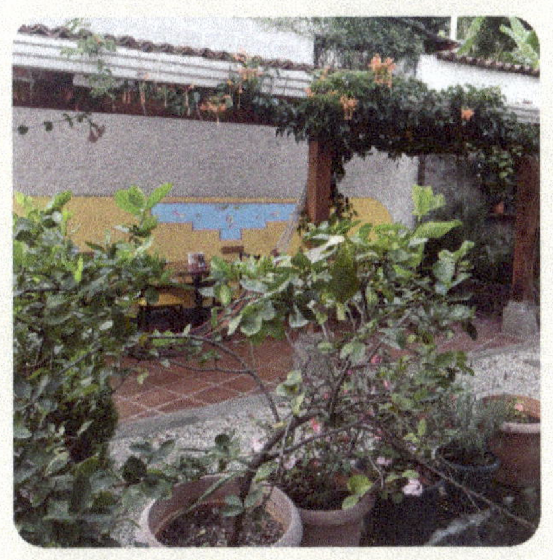

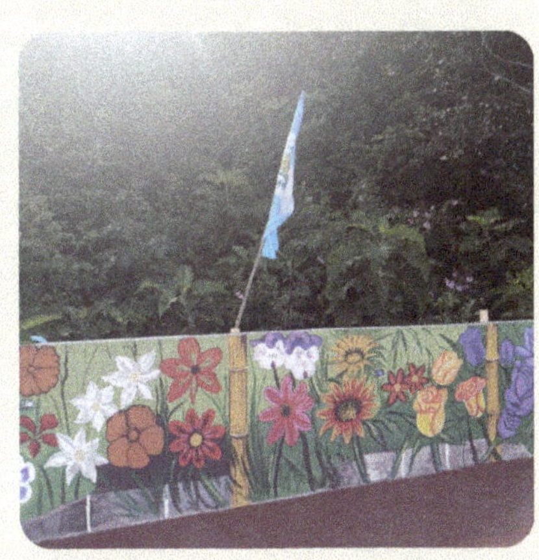

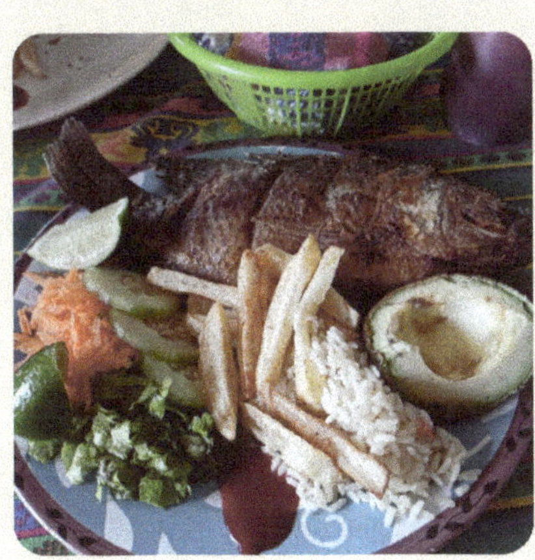

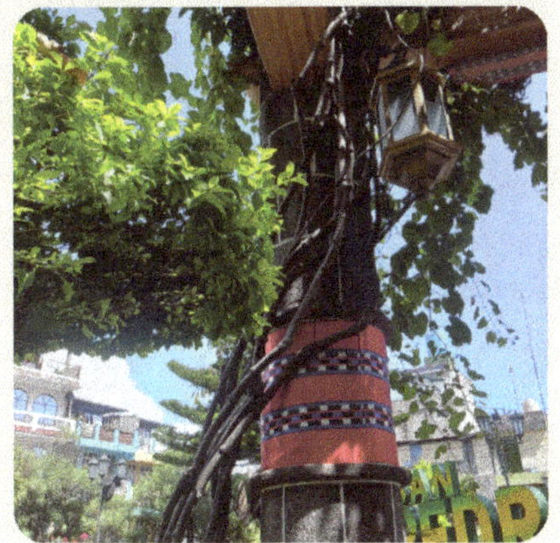

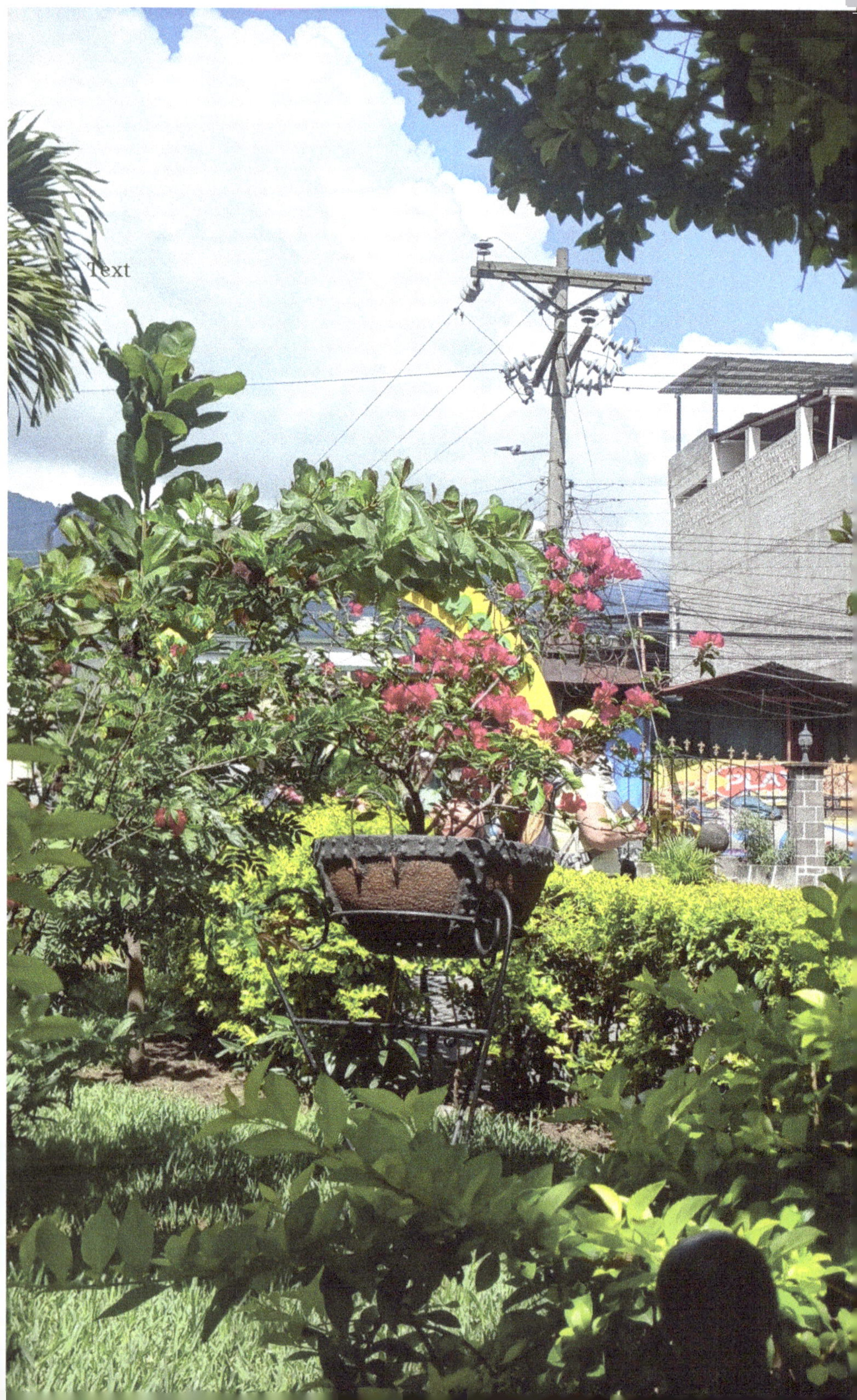
Text

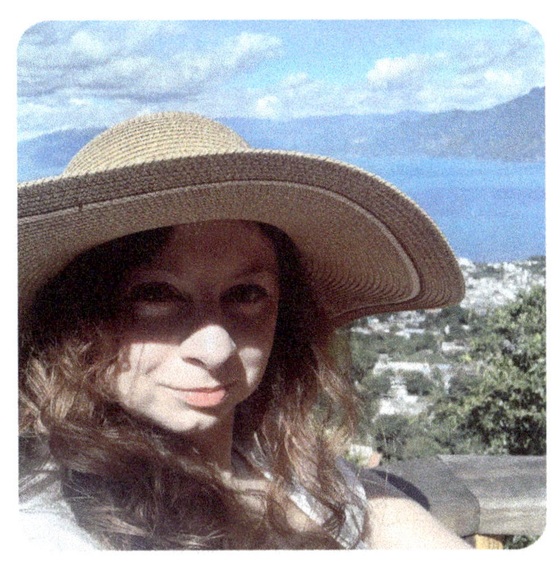

LADY VICTORIA ROSE

CO-OWNER OF ROSE & STONE MEDIA
FOUNDER OF THE COZY FAIRY COLLECTION

Author & Illustrator, Lady Victoria Rose founded *The Cozy Fairy Collection* as a way to share her stories of The 9 Realms of Faery & adventures through the world of humans. She is co-owner of *Rose & Stone Media*, a publishing company on a mission to develop & share the work of independent artists and other overlooked voices. They focus on translations and traditional stories of different regions, and believe in the power of human creativity & collaboration for a better world.

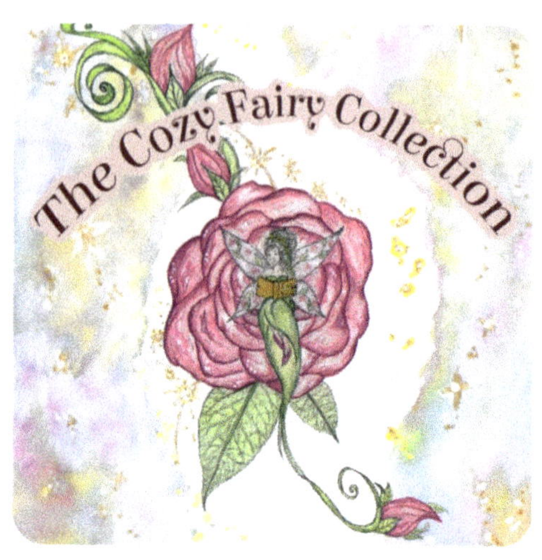

THE COZY FAIRY COLLECTION

Thank you for joining us on this little adventure to wild and wonderful places. This is a very brief overview of a place with a rich history and culture, we hope our stories have been shared and received with all possible love & respect for one another.

If you enjoyed this book, we have an ever growing list of titles from authors of many cultures & genres of every kind, including handmade Miniature Books, ebooks, stationary, and other items. We'd love if you visited

RoseAndStoneMedia.com

to see what new art & adventures are available.

Blessings to all on your journey through life!

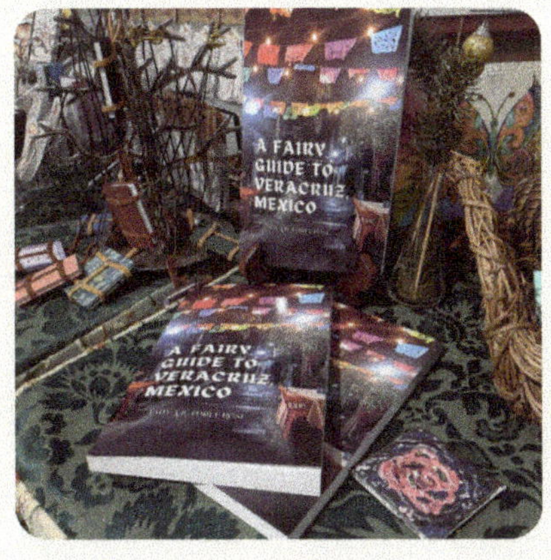

A FAIRY GUIDE TO VERACRUZ MEXICO
A FAIRY GUIDE TO VERACRUZ MEXICO

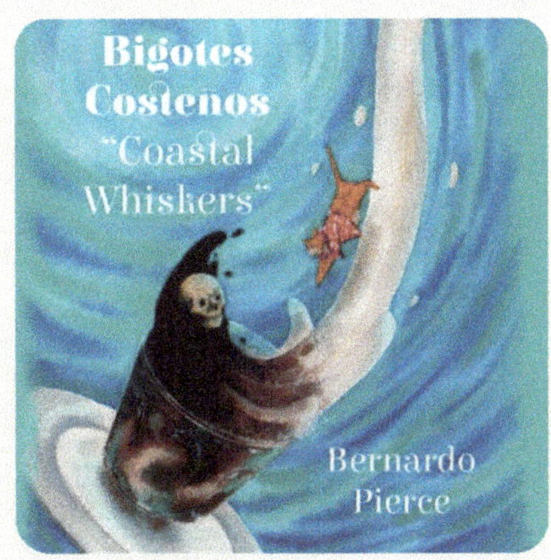

Bigotes Costenos "Coastal Whiskers"
Bernardo Pierce

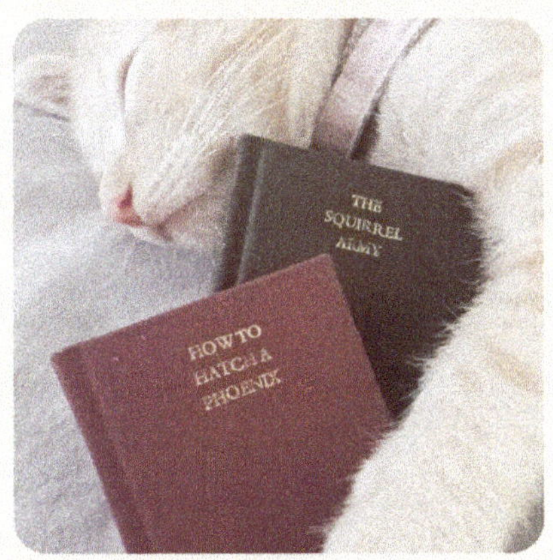

THE SQUIRREL ARMY
HOW TO HATCH A PHOENIX

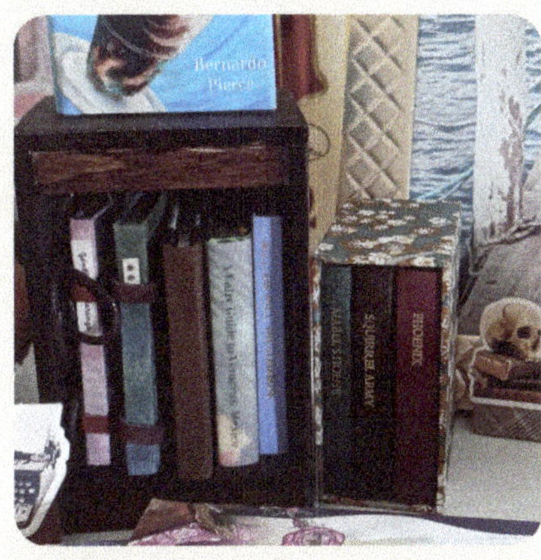

Bernardo Pierce

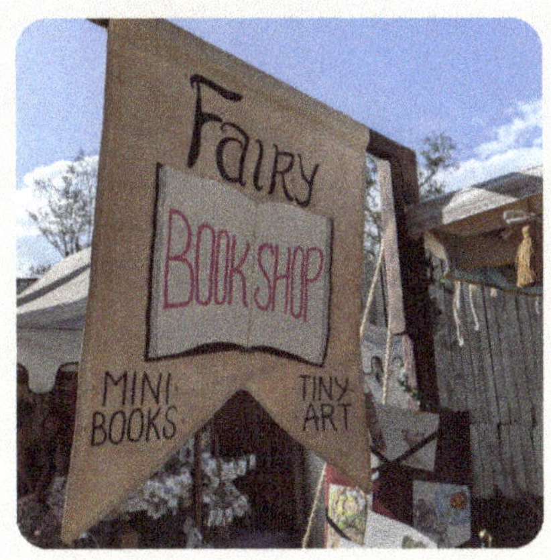

Fairy
BOOK SHOP
MINI BOOKS
TINY ART

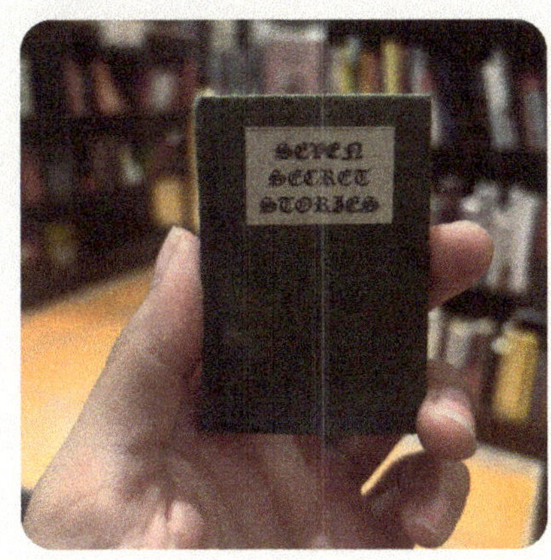

SEVEN SECRET STORIES